Teach'n Beginning Offensive Volleyball Drills, Plays, and Games Free Flow Handbook

By Bob Swope
Series 5, Vol. 17 Free Flow E-Paperback Edition
Copyright 2014 Bob Swope

ISBN 13: 9780991406623

TABLE OF CONTENTS

Note:
This book is a combination of many techniques in several of our books, "Teach'n Volleyball," and "Youth Volleyball Drills and Plays."

1. Warning

If your kids, players on your team, or the participants have any physically limiting conditions, bleeding disorder, high blood pressure, any kind of heart condition, pregnancy or any other condition that may limit them physically, you should have them check with their doctor before letting them participate in any of the drills, plays, games, activities, or exercises discussed in this book.

Be sure participants in these drills, plays, games, or exercises that might even accidentally make hard contact with any of the other participants are all approximately of the same weight and size to avoid a possible accidental serious injury.

All of the drills, plays, exercises, and games for kids discussed in this book should be supervised by a competent adult, coach, or a professional using all the required equipment and safety procedures. **AUTHOR ASSUMES NO LIABILITY FOR ANY ACCIDENTAL INJURY OR EVEN DEATH THAT MAY RESULT FROM USING ANY OF THE VOLLEYBALL TECHNIQUES, DRILLS, OR ACTIVITIES, DISCUSSED IN THIS BOOK.**

Extra care and caution should be taken with any of the drills in this book where players may accidentally get hit with a spiked Volleyball because that may be the more dangerous thing to watch for. Concussions can happen. Occasionally kids will have bruised knees or a broken body part. Remove them and have them immediately checked out by a doctor. Also watch for over exertion (heat stroke and heart problems) to any of your kids or players out on the court that get overheated for some reason. Having a "defibrillator" near by would be a big help in case something like that happens.

Bob Swope
Jacobob Press LLC
Publisher

2. Introduction

My Interest and Intent

Occasionally youth Volleyball coaches have asked me about basic Offensive Volleyball drills, plays, strategies, tactics and games that would be good to have all in one book, to use for training purposes. This handbook is intended to be a supplemental book to my "Teach'n Volleyball" book. It is orientated more for the beginner volleyball coach, rather than parents at home teaching fundamentals. However, parents can help their kids by getting them to work on the drills, plays, tactics, and strategies in this book while at home. We will break this down into where your players are in their training, and what they are doing at that stage of their training.

Also what drills, strategies, plays and tactics to use that will accomplish your goals in teaching them. My suggestion is use the time you have each week to maximize what you want to teach. For the younger 6 -11 years of age kids it's better to break practice drills down into more than one small group to keep everyone busy so that they don't get bored. This is not always easy to do because many coaches only want things done their way, and they don't always trust a helper assistant to do it their way. However, sooner or later you need to trust assistants to help get more done. It's in the best interest of the kids because it's all about the kids not you.

3. Discussion

Training Sessions

Some of the beginning volleyball practices I've seen will only last about an hour. This is where one coach may have the whole group. I have seen coaches spending 10 to 15 minutes warming up, stretching, running and things like that. That leaves only 50 or so minutes to instruct, not counting the water breaks. And it's not-always one-on one instruction. This means you need to manage your time efficiently. You should limit the warm-up and stretching, so you can utilize the maximum amount of practice time. Of course if you have more time its not a problem. The other thing that is important is how many times a week is your practice. If it's only 3 days a week, you better sit down and make a schedule, so you can cover all the things they need to learn. Then follow it. If you have more time, like two hours, you can teach even more fundamentals by adding to our "Sample Practice Schedules" at the back of the book.

Time
Generally, keep your training time to around 10 to 15 minutes per drill being explained, especially if you have a group unless otherwise noted. Now here is where your training techniques may need to change. If you have a helper you can split into two groups. As an example, you might be teaching "forearm passing" and your assistant "pursuing and saving." Then after 10 to 15 minutes you switch or rotate groups. This is because traditionally, there is a lot of techniques to teach to beginning kids. In other words always keep your kids busy doing something at all times except for water breaks. Don't have any kids just standing around waiting because there is only one coach. You don't get as much teaching in that way, within any one practice. Also young kids traditionally get bored easily if you don't keep them busy for the entire training session.

Session Suggestions
I suggest getting as many assistant coaches as you can, then explain to them individually what they are responsible for teaching at their station or group. Tell your staff to learn all the kids names the first day if possible because it helps build a relationship. Time wise plan your whole practice session. The kids will learn more in the short periods of time you have for teaching each day or week. As for the teaching methods we suggest using the "IDEA" slogan approach. **I**ntroduce, **D**emonstrate, **E**xplain what you are teaching, and **A**ttend (answer any question-show them how) to all the players in the group.

The Opponent

If it's possible, it could be beneficial to understand what tendencies your opponent has. Your players need to learn how to quickly figure out what their opponent is doing against them defensively on the other side of the net. Your players should recognize the importance of this strategy, especially after playing an opponent more than once. Here is a little strategy you can employ as their coach. Keep a small pad of paper in your pocket and take notes. Look for weaknesses then when it's game time you can pick the offensive strategies that will attack, counterattack, and defeat what the opponent is doing defensively. Start teaching your young players to have a game plan before they go into a game then test them to make sure and remember what it is. Also have one or two back up plans in case your first plan didn't work and you need to change plans and tactics quickly. And have signals or code words for each one.

Pre Practice/Game Warm Up

Before your team starts to practice or get in a game they need to go through a little warm up to get their muscles warmed up and stretched out. We will give you a nice little quick warm up routine to use. 10 minutes should do it. They need to do this when they first get to the practice. Once your kids learn it, they can do it on their own as a group. If you can teach them to do this well, and look good at it, your opponent may be impressed or intimidated by your teams discipline and focus if they see your team doing this. The organized warm up may put you at an advantage, as your opponent's may be a little psyched out.

Drills

I am going to refer to the drills as "Skill Training Activities" because that's what they really are. Also I am going to throw in a newer term now being used a lot. It is called "Core Training." What it does is train their body to automatically make certain moves that will make them a better player. Drills will be organized by *"numbers"* so that your assistant coaches can use them and become more familiar with them that way. This way you are all on the same page as they say.

Techniques

Techniques are the most important fundamental things to learn. For easy reference the techniques will be organized by "*numbers*" also. They will be arranged in the different offensive techniques and tactics. Each technique or tactic will have a short explanation for how it is supposed to work, strong points, what it is designed to accomplish.

Game Type Scrimmages

It's a good idea to introduce game type scrimmages once in a while. Beginners sometimes have a tendency to get bored with constant drilling. They want to see what it's like to go out and play in a game against an actual opponent. You need to referee these games though just like in a real game. Just don't get frustrated by expecting perfect play by beginners. Have several spotters, each watching some particular aspect of their offensive play, and taking notes. As they get better you can be more particular about calling scores and penalties.

Core Training Games

Many coaches over the years have asked me to give them some "core training" games they can have the kids play once in a while at practices. Not just any games though, but games that will help develop some part of their "core training" and "muscle memory" in a particular skill. So we are adding some games that will do just that. For easy reference these games will be organized by "*numbers*" also. Some of the time it's hard for coaches to buy into these games, but the more you play them, the more you will see your player's agility, speed and skills improving. Each game will have a short explanation for how it is supposed to work, strong points, and what the game is designed to accomplish.

General Strategies and Tactics

The first general strategy I recommend is "have a game plan" to match your team with their opponent. Try to watch the opponent warming up, and make some notes. Remember though these are only kids, so coach accordingly with your strategies and tactics if you are working with kids

7-11 years of age. You know the old "KISS" (Keep-It-Simple-Stupid) phrase. In volleyball it is not structured as say football with all its many plays. However, each player does have a roll to play depending on their position on the court. For beginners it's important to teach them in detail what their individual role is at each position and how it relates to the team. For the in-depth strategies see the full "Strategies" section.

4. Warm Up Exercises

I'm going to give you a quick warm up routine your players can use to get warmed up and their muscles stretched. That's all young kids really need. Teach your players how to do these group exercises all by themselves as a group. It will be easier that way. Here is an idea I have used before. When you are warming up your team, you can try this. Have your captain or a respected teammate stand in front of the group, and lead the routine. Teach your players to count slowly and out loud. The team alternates counting, when the leaders yell. "One," the group yells, "Two on the next rep," etc. You only need to do six reps of each exercise. It's also a "psyche out" for any opponent's that may be watching. And you may need this edge if the opponent's are more experienced or have stronger players. You are only looking at about 10 minutes to go through these.

The Simple Routine
1. Start by doing 10 jumping jacks to get their muscles warmed up.
2. Next slowly do 6 "seated hamstring/quadriceps stretches.
3. Next slowly do 3 pelvic stretches on each side, holding for 3 seconds between them.
4. Next slowly do 6 push forward pull back ankle stretches.
5. Next slowly do 3 front quadriceps stretches on both thighs, leaning forward and holding for 3 seconds between them.
6. Next slowly do 6 rear shoulder stretches, holding for 3 seconds.

7. Next slowly do 3 front shoulder stretches on each shoulder, holding for 3 seconds between them.
8. Last use a teammate to lean on, or find a wall, and slowly do 3 calf stretches on each leg, holding it for 3 seconds between each rep.

Jumping Jacks   Hamstrings /Quads   Pelvics   Ankles

Front Quadriceps   Rear Shoulders   Front Shoulder   Calf

5. Where They Play on the Court

This is basically for new beginning coaches without a lot of experience in volleyball. In youth volleyball there are usually 6 players and positions on the volleyball court for each team (side). In some places they will occasionally play 3 vs 3 volleyball. And in beach volleyball they will sometimes play 2 vs 2 volleyball. In this book we will only cover 6 vs 6 volleyball because it is the most popular. Volleyball is not like some of the other sports that play on a court. They start out arranged in a certain order at the time of the serve, which starts out play *(SEE DIAGRAM 1)*.

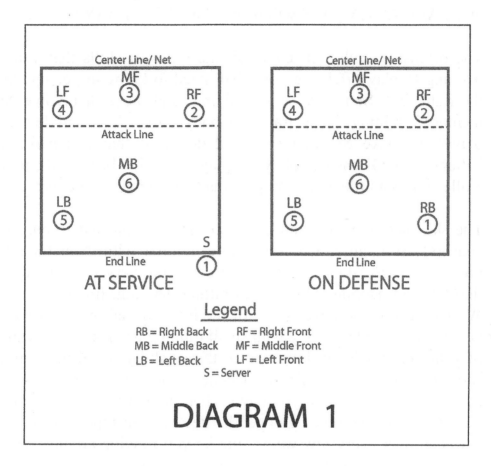

DIAGRAM 1

And after the point has been made each player rotates around clockwise to the next position. As an example, No.1 moves to No. 6, No.2 moves to No. 1. At the serve the server usually is right behind the end line. All the other players have to be within the court lines until the ball has been served. In youth volleyball there are 6 players on the court for offensive play. There are many different locations where the coach may move them up or back once the ball is in play. We will just give you the required positions and when they start play.

6. Offensive Skill Training Activities

Note: ALL ACTIVITIES will be numbered for "EASY " reference.

The offensive drills will cover all the types of skills that young kids learning to play offensive volleyball need to know to get started of on the right foot. Some are "core training' and most all involve "muscle memory" training. They train the body, arms, legs and feet of your players to make certain moves and decisions that will make them a better player. Offensive volleyball players need to be poised and patient. Volleyball is a little more complex than a beginner would expect.

The skill activities are numbered so that you can have your assistant coach(s) use them and become more familiar with them for reference purposes. These skill activities will cover the very basic fundamentals like forearm passing, spiking and hitting, serving, tipping, and setting. We will also try to cover some of the little special techniques that will help them. The plan is stay with small training groups, where you or one of your coaches is teaching one of theses skills. Keep the time period short, maybe 10 to 15 minutes depending on the size of your team and how much practice time you have. Then blow a whistle and one group moves over to the other group. The key is keep repeating the training over and over every few weeks, but keep it moving around to different techniques. Not only the same ones all the time.

Modern volleyball training, and conditioning, is advancing all the time. In this book we will try to follow the latest recommended techniques, and tailor them for the younger kids. I will break the drills and skill training down into the fundamental categories, and how they relate to what you want to teach. We will use picture figures, and diagrams as much as possible, to eliminate some of the confusion for all helping fathers, and some mothers, who may never have played the game of volleyball. So, bear with us, those of you that have played a lot of volleyball. This book was basically written as a reference book for beginners, both parents and coaches.

The size of your groups will depend on how many kids you have at your training session, and how many instructors (coaches) you have. As an example if you have 12 kids on your team, then you could have 2 groups of 6. Then you would need 2 stations and at least one instructor, coach, or parent per group. The bigger your group is though the more problems you will have. Smaller groups mean more touches, and more teaching control on you or your coaches part. However, some drills may need to be combined into the whole team in order to teach similar techniques more smoothly and quicker to the team as a whole.

If you can find them, have an instructor and an assistant at each station, then show them what to do. Most coaches don't like to do this even if they may need to because of a large group size, but using parents as assistants and showing them exactly what you want them to do can work. I do this all the time and it works great for me with young kids. Parents are usually just sitting around watching with nothing to do anyway, so why not get them involved and put them to work. There is always some of them that are willing to help. You would be surprised at how many parents are willing to help, not a lot but quite a few. And that's all you need. The key is just show them *EXACTLY* what you want them to do.

Here is another technique that works great with young kids. They have a short attention span. So when you need to talk to all of them, then make them all sit down cross legged on the ground in a semi circle in front of you. When you do it this way, they have less of a tendency to mess around, especially with boys, who tend talk too much when you are talking. Don't let them stand up, that's when the listening usually tends to stop and distractions set in.

Additional Help for Activities

If you are a beginning coach, and you are having trouble understanding how to implement these offensive activities in more detail, get a copy of the "Teach'n Volleyball" book. This is our teaching book for Volleyball, and it goes into a little more detail on exactly how to teach kids the particular skill we are discussing.

Legend for All Diagrams
(Unless otherwise spelled out in the diagram or section)

SV = Server	LF = Left Front Player	◯ = Offensive Player
SE = Setter	RB = Right Back Player	▢ = Defensive Player
P = Players	MB = Middle Back Player	X = Defending Position
H = Hitter (Spiker)	LB = Left Back Player	● = Starting Position
B = Blocker	F = Faking Player	⊗ = Coach
RF = Right Front Player		
MF = Middle Front Player		

⟶ or ⟶ = Player Movement
- - -➤ = Path of Passed Ball
——➤ = Path of Served Ball
⊕ = Ball
♟ = Cones

7. Individual Footwork and Movement Techniques

The first fundamental your players need to learn is the basic footwork and movements in volleyball. They have to do them enough so they become a habit with them (muscular memory). These drills are basically to teach them to move automatically to the ball. The footwork and movements put the player in the right position to execute whatever skill they need, to make a play on the ball. The "hop" part of the technique is probably the hardest part for young kids to learn. They usually make too small of a "hop," or none at all.

There are four basic fundamental movements. Leap hopping, slide stepping, crossover stepping, and the spike approach steps. The crossover step is a blocking footwork move. What this means is you

12

probably don't need to teach this move until your players can get their hands over the top of the net. We will break all the movements down separately. Eventually though your players will need to learn all of them.

Skill Activity No. 25, 26- The Leap Hopping Technique
Object of the Activity:
Teach all your players how to move quickly and get into a balanced position by using leap hopping.
What you will need:
You will need some room on a back corner of the court or in front of the net, 2 coaches, and a whistle.
The Basics are:
A. This is basically taking one step forward with the *right* foot, followed quickly with a jump up forward hop coming down in a balanced position on the *left* foot, and almost simultaneously followed by the *right* foot. It should make a step "pop," then a quick "pop"- "pop" sound on the floor as the feet come down each time *(SEE FIGURE 25-A)*.

B. Next take a step backward with the *right* foot, followed quickly with a jump up backward hop coming down in a balanced position on the *left* foot, and almost simultaneously followed by the *right* foot. It should make a step "pop," then a quick "pop"- "pop" sound on the floor as the feet come down each time *(SEE FIGURE 25-B)*.

C. This is basically taking one step forward with the *left* foot, followed quickly with a jump up forward hop coming down in a balanced position on the *right* foot, and almost simultaneously followed by the *left* foot. It should make a step "pop," then a quick "pop"- "pop" sound on the floor as the feet come down each time *(SEE FIGURE 25-C)*.

D. Next take a step backward with the *left* foot, followed quickly with a jump up backward hop coming down in a balanced position on the *right* foot, and almost simultaneously followed by the *left* foot. It should make a step "pop," then a quick "pop"- "pop" sound on the floor as the feet come down each time *(SEE FIGURE 25-D)*.

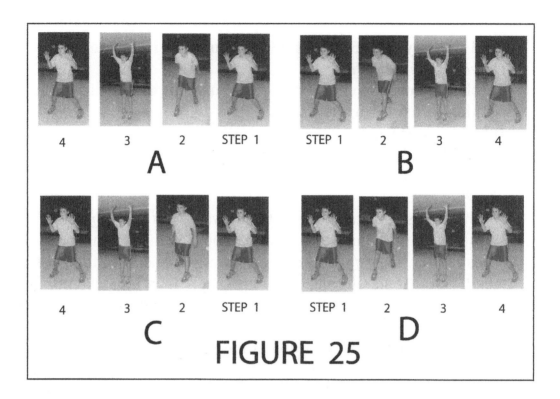

FIGURE 25

Working the Activity:
This can be practiced out in the back yard, but it's better to work on a driveway, or a gym floor. The reason is, you can hear the "pops" especially on the gym floor as the feet come down. Then you know they are doing it correctly. If they don't jump up and hop, you will not hear the "pops" of the feet. Have them get into a ready position first *(SEE FIGURE 26),* then go through the *right* foot leap hops at least 5 times each at a session, forward then backward. Next have them go through the *left* foot leap hops at least 5 times each at a session, forward then backward *(SEE FIGURE 25)*. To make it easier to learn have them go through each step in slow motion first, stopping at each position. Then check each position to make sure they have it right.

14

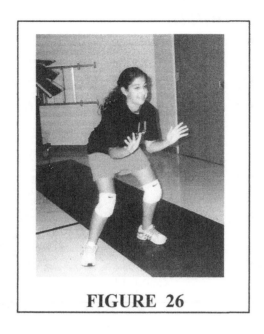

FIGURE 26

Emphasize:
Going slowly through each position first then jumping up hopping fast and hearing the popping.
Run the Activity:
Run this activity quickly over and over for about 15 minutes.

Skill Activity No. 27- The Slide Stepping Technique
Object of the Activity:
Teach all your players how to move sideways quickly by using the slide stepping technique.
What you will need:
You will need some room on a back corner of the court or in front of the net, 2 coaches, and a whistle.
The Basics are:
    A. This is basically taking a step to the <u>right</u> with the right foot, then sliding the left foot over to it. Next make a short step "hop" over to the right, with the right foot first, coming down in a balanced

position with the feet under the shoulders *(SEE FIGURE 27-GOING RIGHT)*.

B. Next take a step to the *left* with the left foot, then sliding the right foot over to it. Next make a short step "hop" over to the left, with the left foot first, coming down in a balanced position with the feet under the shoulders *(SEE FIGURE 27-GOING LEFT)*.

GOING RIGHT

GOING LEFT

FIGURE 27

Working the Activity:
This can be practiced out in the back yard, but it's better to work on a driveway, or a gym floor. The reason is, you can hear the "pops" when the feet come down, especially on the gym floor. Then you know they are doing it correctly. If they don't jump up and hop, you will not hear the "pops" of the feet. Have them get into a ready position first *(SEE FIGURE 26),* then go through the slide step to the *right* first for at least 5 times a session in slow motion. Next have them go through the slide step to the *left* for at least 5 times a session in slow motion *(SEE FIGURE 27)*. Then keep speeding it up until they have it right.

16

Emphasize:

Going through all the moves first in slow motion, then jumping up and going sideways fast through all the moves and hearing the popping.

Run the Activity:

Run this activity quickly over and over for about 15 minutes.

Skill Activity No. 28- The Crossover Stepping Technique

Object of the Activity:

Teach all your players how to move sideways quickly by using the cross over stepping technique.

What you will need:

You will need some room on a back corner of the court or in front of the net, 2 coaches, and a whistle.

The Basics are:

    A. To go to the right, turn to the right with the body, and open to the right with the right foot turning it 90 degrees to the right. Next take a quick big crossover step in front with the left foot. Step and swing the right leg around to the front, squaring the body to the front, all in one move *(SEE FIGURE 28-A)*.

    B. To go to the left, turn to the left with the body, and open to the left with the left foot turning it 90 degrees to the left. Next take a quick big crossover step in front with the right foot. Step and swing the left leg around to the front, squaring the body to the front, all in one move *(SEE FIGURE 28-B)*.

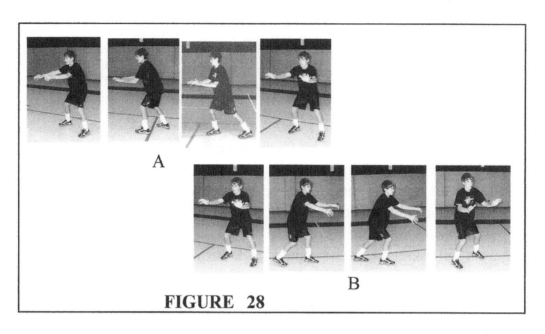

FIGURE 28

Working the Activity:

This can be practiced out in the back yard, but it's better to work on a driveway, or a gym floor. The reason is, you can hear a slight "pop" when the feet come down, especially on the gym floor. Then you know they are doing it correctly. If they don't jump up at least a little bit you won't hear the "pop" of the feet. Have them get into a ready position first *(SEE FIGURE 26),* then go through the crossover step to the <u>right</u> for at least 5 times in slow motion at a session. Next have them go through the crossover step to the <u>left </u> for at least 5 times in slow motion at a session *(SEE FIGURE 28).*

Emphasize:

Going through all the crossing the feet over in slow motion, then going sideways fast, and hearing the slight popping.

Run the Activity:

Run this activity quickly over and over for about 15 minutes.

Skill Activity No. 29- The Two Step Spike Approach Footwork Technique

Object of the Activity:

Teach all your players how to make a quick two step approach to spiking the ball.

What you will need:

You will need some room on a back corner of the court or in front of the net, 2 coaches, and a whistle.

The Basics are:

This approach is for quick spikes on balls that have been set maybe a foot or so above the net. Work on this only with kids that can jump above the net though. Not the real little kids. The player leap hops forward, landing first with foot on the side of the spiking arm, then in quick succession the other foot. This is where the technique gets its name. After landing with the second foot they push off and jump up for the spike.

| Jump | Step 2 | Step 1 | Start |

FIGURE 29

Working the Activity:

To practice this technique, you probably want to take your player out to where there is a net in front of them. This way they get the feel of where the net is. They don't have to jump as high as they can, to practice this footwork, just up enough to get the feel of going up. Again this is building "muscle memory." Starting from the ready position *(SEE FIGURE 26)* have them make at least 2 of these jumps at a training session in slow motion first , then fast *(SEE FIGURE 29)*.

Emphasize:

Dipping at their knees then a big, from way back, arm swing followed by the push off and jump up.

Run the Activity:

Run this activity quickly over and over for about 15 minutes.

Skill Activity No. 30- The Three Step Spike Approach Footwork Technique

Object of the Activity:

Teach all your players how to make a quick three step approach to spiking the ball.

What you will need:

You will need some room on a back corner of the court or in front of the net, 2 coaches, and a whistle.

The Basics are:

This approach is for when the spiker has a little more time than with a quick spike. Work on this only with kids that can jump above the net though. Not the real little kids. The player first takes a normal step forward with the foot on the opposite side as the spiking arm. Next they leap hop forward landing first on the foot on the same side of the spiking arm, then in quick succession the other foot. These 3 steps is where the technique gets its name. After landing with the second foot they push off and jump up for the spike.

Start   Step 1   2   3   Jump

FIGURE 30

Working the activity:

To practice this technique, you probably want to take your player out to where there is a net in front of them. This way they get the feel of where the net is. They don't have to jump as high as they can, to practice this footwork, just up enough to get the feel of going up. Again this is building "muscle memory". Starting from the ready position *(SEE FIGURE 26)* have them make at least 3 of these jumps in slow motion at a training session, then go fast *(SEE FIGURE 30)*.

Emphasize:

Dipping at their knees then a big, from way back, arm swing followed by the push off and jump up. Going through the moves in slow motion first.

Run the Activity:

Run this activity quickly over and over for about 15 minutes.

Skill Activity No. 31- The Four Step Spike Approach Technique
Object of the Activity:

Teach all your players how to make a quick four step approach to spiking the ball.

What you will need:

You will need some room on a back corner of the court or in front of the net, 2 coaches, and a whistle.

The Basics are:

This approach is for when the spiker wants to go way up in the air for a high set ball. Work on this only with kids that can jump above the net though. Not the real little kids. The player first takes a short step forward with the foot on the side of the spiking arm. Next they take a great big step with the foot on the side opposite of the spiking arm. Following that, they push off and leap hop forward landing first on the foot on the side of the spiking arm, then in quick succession the other foot. These 4 steps is where the technique gets it's name. After landing with the second foot on the leap hop, they push off and jump up for the spike.

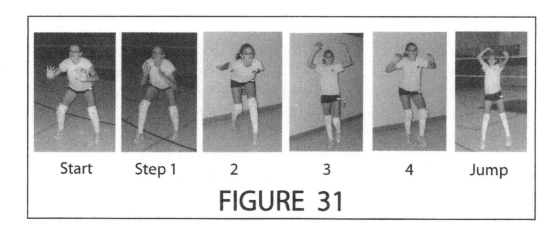

| Start | Step 1 | 2 | 3 | 4 | Jump |

FIGURE 31

Working the Activity:

To practice this technique, you probably want to take your player out to where there is a net in front of them. This way they get the feel of where the net is. They probably want to jump a little bit higher on the 4 step, but not as high as they can. Maybe up about 75 percent of their maximum height. Again this is building "muscle memory" for the steps. Starting from the ready position *(SEE FIGURE 26)* have them make at

22

least 3 of these jumps in slow motion at a training session, then fast *(SEE FIGURE 31*

Emphasize:

Dipping at their knees then a big, from way back, arm swing followed by the push off and jump up.

Run the Activity:

Run this activity quickly over and over for about 15 minutes.

Skill Activity No. 32- The Side Step Spike Approach Technique

Object of the Activity:

Teach all your players how to make a quick side step approach to spiking the ball. This is to fool and get away from a blocker.

What you will need:

You will need some room on a back corner of the court or in front of the net, 2 coaches, and a whistle.

The Basics are:

This approach is for when the spiker wants to fool the blocker, and shift to the side of them, to get a clear space to make the hit on the ball. Work on this only with kids that can jump above the net though. Not the real little kids. The player first takes a step forward towards the blocker with the foot on the side of the spiking arm. Next they take a step forward towards the blocker with the opposite foot. Then they pivot and step to the side, parallel with the net direction, first with the foot that is out in front. Then they step with the opposite foot in the same direction. As this leg makes the plant, they pivot back towards the front, push off on it and jump up to make the spike. The fake to the front, and switch to the side, is where the technique gets its name.

Working the Activity:

To practice this technique, you probably want to take your player out to where there is a net in front of them. This way they get the feel of where the net is. They don't have to jump as high as they can, to practice this footwork, just up enough to get the feel of going up. Again this is building "muscle memory" for the steps. Starting from the ready position *(SEE FIGURE 26)* have them make at least 3 of these jumps in slow motion to the right *(SEE FIGURE 32-A),* and 3 to the left in slow motion, then fast *(SEE FIGURE 32-B)* at a training session.

| Jump | Turn | Side 1 Step | Pivot | 2 Steps | Start |

A

| Start | 2 Steps | Pivot | Side 1 Step | Turn | Jump |

B

FIGURE 32

Emphasize:
The quick pivot and the turn to get to the side and away quickly from the blocker. Going through the moves in slow motion first.
Run the Activity:
Run this activity quickly over and over for about 15 minutes.

Team Footwork Drills

These are drills you can run with the whole team involved. You keep running these drills every once in a while to sharpen up the footwork of all your players.

The Footwork Drill (No. 300)
Object of the Activity:
Teach all your players to further sharpen up all their footwork skill moves.
What you will need:
You will need a whole half court, 2 coaches, and a whistle.
The Basics are:
This is sharpening up their footwork skills for "leap hopping," "Slide Stepping," "Crossover Stepping," "The 2, 3 , and 4 Step Spike Approach," and the "Side Step Spike Approach."

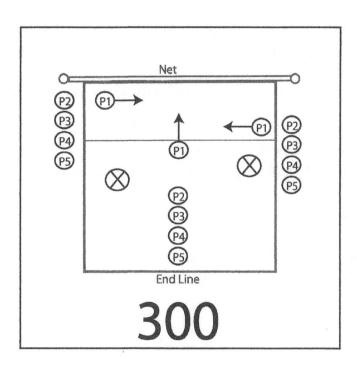

Working the Activity:

Have your players line up in 3 groups. Player P1 in the center group starts out on the whistle. They do 1 or 2 "leap hops" straight ahead then go to the end of the line one their right. Coach blows their whistle and player P1 in the line on the left does "slide steps" all the way across to the other side then goes to the end of the line in the middle. Coach blows their whistle again and player P1 on the line on the right does a "crossover" step all the way to the other side than goes to the end of the line on the left side.

This is how players rotate and do a different step each time. After everyone has been through these 3 moves once coach blows their and everyone stops. Now coach picks 3 different footwork moves for each of the 3 lines. The slide and side stepping moves come from the sides, from the middle line. If players are having trouble with the footwork have the roving coach pull them aside and work with them on their moves. This way the drill keeps going.

Emphasize:

The players going through the steps quickly so that the drill keeps going and does no slow down. You get more training in that way

Run the Activity:

You may need to run this drill quickly over and over for about 45 minutes.

The Setters Footwork Drills (No.24)

Object of the drill: Have all your setter's work on their footwork moves

What you will need: You will need a half court with a net and a cart of balls.

Working the drill: There are four variations of this drill. One the perfect pass, two backing up, three is four-steps off, and four is two-steps off.

1. PERFECT PASS

Setter doesn't have to move to get to the ball. Coach makes a perfect lob pass up in the air to them, just a little bit in front of them.

2. BACKING UP

Setter has to back up using back stepping. Coach makes the lob pass just a little behind them so that they need to back up.

3. FOUR-STEPS OFF

Setter needs to make four shuffle steps forward to get under the ball. Coach makes the lob pass about four steps out in front of the setter.

4. TWO-STEPS OFF

Setter needs to make two shuffle steps forward to get under the ball. Coach makes the lob pass about two steps out in front of the setter.

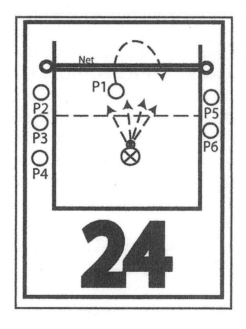

Emphasize:

Making the correct footwork moves for each of the four toss lobs.

Run this drill:
Let each player have one try at each of the four moves, then switch and rotate players. Have players get quickly into position so that the drill runs rapidly and smoothly. Run it for only 30 minutes then they move to the next station or drill activity.

8. Individual Passing Techniques

The forearm pass is a technique for getting the ball to another teammate, or receiving spikes and serves from the opponent. This is also a good technique to use for balls that have gone into the net. A good forearm pass to the "setter" will help set up spikes and kills. When little kids first start to use this technique, they might complain about stinging on their arms. Have them learn to soften and catch the ball on hard hit balls, by not swinging the arms at the ball.

To get ready for making a forearm pass, the have to first learn to get into the "ready" position *(SEE FIGURE 26)*. The hands have to be held in a certain way, to make what is called a "platform". If a team does not have players with good passing technique skills, it makes it easier for the opposition to score points. One of the most important things for your player to learn is, get to the ball quickly. Use the "leap hop" technique for the footwork. Tell them NOT to swing at the ball, just let it come down on their forearms then direct it.

Skill Activity No. 52, 53, 54, 55- The Forearm Pass Technique
Object of the Drill: Teach your players how to make forearm passes to teammates.
What you will Need: You will need half a court with a net to work on, 2 coaches, and a whistle.
The Basics Are: This is a method of putting their hands together at the wrists and using them as a platform to catch and pass the ball to a teammate.

The forearm pass is a technique where the arms are held together at the wrists to form a kind of shelf to catch the ball *(SEE FIGURE 52)*. The position of the hands is very important to learn so that the arms do not come apart when a player is making contact with the ball. Also this makes a flat surface with the forearms, to form the shelf. First place the thumbs on both hands next to each other. Next wrap all the fingers on the right hand together and grip them around and over the top of the left hand. Then all the fingers together on the left hand wrap around and grip the bottom of the right hand *(SEE FIGURE 53)*.

FIGURE 52

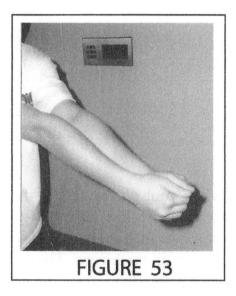

FIGURE 53

The "platform tilt" is a part of the forearm passing technique that lets the player direct the pass right to the place they intend it to go to. To accomplish this they have to get into position to face the target, or player they wish the pass to go to. The "tilt" comes from the shifting of the body and feet to make the catch of the ball. The arms forming the platform remain flat, but the body tilts and the feet shift to direct the ball *(SEE FIGURE 54)*. The angle at which the ball comes off the platform is what directs the pass.

FIGURE 54

When your player gets to the ball, they should make contact above the wrists and below the elbows *(SEE FIGURE 55-B)*. Teach them to shift or move their body so they <u>do not</u> make contact way up above the elbows on the biceps. They should also be in a position to make contact at or below the waist, and not way up high by the chest. The arms are extended, and the elbows locked. Make a catch and lift of the ball, and not a swing at it type of movement. The lift is accomplished, from the squat position, by straightening out the legs and coming up on the balls of the feet *(SEE FIGURE 55-C)*.

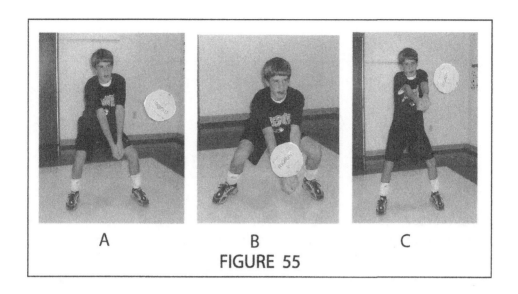

A   B   C

FIGURE 55

Working the Activity:

To practice the forearm pass, take them out to the back yard or the court. If you can find a net, the drill will be more beneficial. This is because you can set up pass situations like in a real game. As an example, have them get anywhere in the back row *(SEE FIGURE 51)*. Then you, mom or dad, go to the other side of the net and throw the ball over the net to them. You will probably need 1 or 2 friends to help out on this drill. What your player needs to do is, go to the ball when it comes over the net.

Have the friend(s) get in the front row, up near the net, on the same side as your player. When the ball gets to them they forearm pass it to the friend. Have the friend or teammate move from side to side, or have them pass it first to one helper then the other. Watch them closely after you throw the ball, and make sure they are correctly lifting the ball and not hitting at it. Also coach, mom, or dad, don't always throw the ball over the net right to them. Make them move around to get to the ball. They should make at least 6 of these passes at a training session.

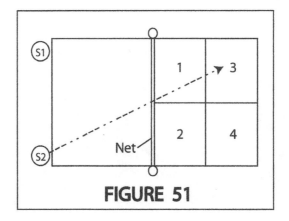

FIGURE 51

Emphasize:
Getting their wrists together, making a good platform, and learning to direct the ball to where they want it to go.

Run this drill: Let each player have at least 2 tries at each at making a good platform and correctly directing their pass. Run it for only 30 minutes then they move to the next station or drill activity.

Team Passing Drills

These are drills you can run with the whole team involved. You keep running these drills every once in a while to sharpen up the footwork of all your players.

The Basic Forearm Pass Drill (No.10)
Object of the drill:
Learn the basic forearm passing technique.
What you will need:
You will need a volleyball court and a cart of balls, or a you can just go about anyplace inside or outside where there is some room to pass the ball around. The court works best though because you can set up situations like a real game, and it lends more of a game feel.

Working the drill:
Either demonstrate or remind your players how the technique works with their arms. Have your players pair off about 10 feet apart from backcourt to front court in a row. One player lobs the ball to their partner, the partner forearm passes the ball back to them, then they forearm pass it back. Then it keeps going back and forth.

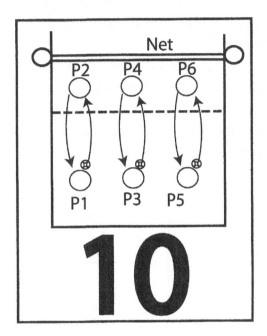

Emphasize:
The twisting of the body to line up the direction the pass needs to go. Also a soft lift of the arms, not a big hard swinging hit. Just enough to get the ball to where they want it to go works best, not way over targets head.

Run this drill:
Let the back and forth go on for about 8 minutes then stop. Briefly remind them how to do it again. They rest a few minutes then start up again. Run the drill for only 15 minutes, then have them move to the next station or start a different drill.

The Basic Overhead Pass Drill (No.11)

Object of the drill:

Learn the basic technique of overhead passing.

What you will need:

You can use the volleyball court and a cart of balls, or you can just go about anyplace inside or outside where there is some room to pass the ball around. The court works best though because you can set up situations like a real game, and it has game feel.

Working the drill:

Either demonstrate or remind your players how the technique works with their hands and arms. Have your players pair off about 10 feet apart from backcourt to front court in a row. One player lobs the ball to their partner, the partner overhead passes the ball back to them, then they overhead pass it back.

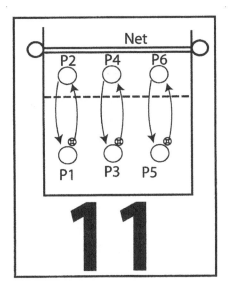

Emphasize:

How the wrists are cocked back and the fingers are spread and relaxed about 4 to 8 inches above the forehead. Also they shape their hands like the volleyball in front of their forehead and look through the window formed by the thumb and forefingers.

Run this drill:

Let the back and forth go on for about 8 minutes then stop. Briefly remind them how to do it again. They rest a few minutes then start up again. Run the drill for only 15 minutes, then have them move to the next station or start a different drill.

The Shuffle Step Passing Drill (No.12)
Object of the drill:

They learn the basic technique of shuffle stepping sideways to get to the ball, then pass it back to the tosser.

What you will need:

You can use the volleyball court and a cart of balls, or you can just go about anyplace inside or outside where there is some room to pass the ball around. The court works best though because you can set up situations more like a real game, and it has game feel.

Working the drill:

Either demonstrate or remind your players how the technique works with their shuffling over to the ball. Have your players P1 and P2 pair off about 10 feet apart from backcourt to front court. Player P1 lobs the ball high in the air to a spot away from P2, then P2 quickly shuffles over and forearm passes it back to P1.

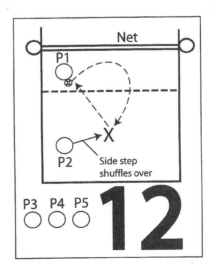

Emphasize:
Quick shuffle side stepping over to the spot where the ball will come down, then square up to P1 and forearm pass it back to them. Two toss passes then P1 and P2 switch places for two more passes. Then they go to the end of the line. Two new players quickly move up, the activity repeats itself.

Run this drill: Two toss-passes for each pair, then rotate. Run the drill for only 15 minutes, then have them move to the next station or start a different drill.

The Passing to the Setter Drill (No.13)
Object of the drill:
They learn to quickly get to the ball, square up, then pass it to the setter.
What you will need:
You will need a volleyball court and net, a cart of balls, and a stand or chair for this drill.
Working the drill:
Either demonstrate or remind your players how they need to get quickly to the ball, then use the appropriate pass method to quickly pass the ball

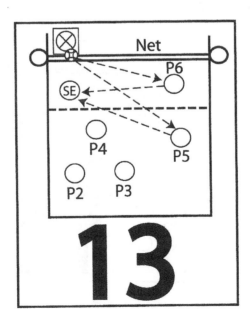

over to the setter. Coach can throw or lob the ball somewhere near anyone of the players. Mix it up. Setter just drops the ball out of the way after they get the pass. A feeder gives a new ball to the coach right after they throw or lob. This keeps the drill moving. Rotate the setter after all the other players have passed to them once.

Emphasize:

Getting a good pass to the setter, either forearm or overhead, that they can handle. This is so that they can get under the ball, and get a nice high pass to a hitter as if it was in a real game.

Run this drill:

Run the drill for only 15 minutes, then have them move to the next station or start another drill. Coach needs mix up who you lob or throw to.

The Quick Shuffle Passing Drill (No.14)

Object of the drill:

Learn the basic technique of quick forearm passing.

What you will need:

You can use the volleyball court, a cart of balls, and a feeder. Or you can just go about anyplace inside or outside where there is some room to pass the ball around. The court works best though because you get the feel of a real game.

Working the drill:

Either demonstrate or remind your players how the technique of shuttle sliding across is going to work. Have 3 players get in the front row about 10 feet apart from P4 in the backcourt. P1 lobs the ball out in front of the sliding P4. They forearm pass the ball to P2, then keep sliding sideways. P2 lobs the ball right back. Then they forearm pass the ball to P3, who lobs it right back to them. P4 then takes the ball, goes to the end of the line, and gives the ball to the feeder. As soon as P3 gets the pass, P5 moves up gets a lob, passes and shuttles across the same way. Then P6 and so on. Every player goes through twice then P1, P2, and P3 rotate and switch with P4, P5, and P6. Then they start through again. A feeder keeps giving a ball to the P1 position so that the drill keeps moving.

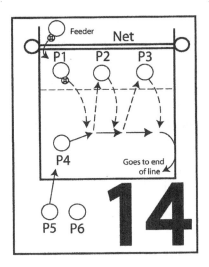

Emphasize:
Good quick lobs, and passers shuttling and sliding through quickly. Rotating, switching, and feeding has to move quickly also.
Run this drill:
Run it for only 15 minutes then have them move to the next station or a different drill.

The Over the Net Fast Pace Passing Drill (No.15)
Object of the drill:
Learn make a lot of passes rapidly over the net in a short period of time.
What you will need:
You can use the volleyball court with a net, a cart of balls, and a feeder.
Working the drill:
Either demonstrate or remind your players how the drill is going to work. Have 2 players get on one side of the net and 1 player on the other side of the net. P3 lobs or throws the ball to P1 over in the back court. They forearm pass the ball to P2 up in front of the net in the center setters position. P2 bounce passes the ball under the net to P3. As

soon as they throw or pass the ball, the feeder hands P3 another ball. They immediately lob or pass the ball to P1 again. This puts two balls into play to keep the drill going rapid fire. After 3 passes P1 goes to the end of the line, and P4 quickly moves in to take their place, and the drill keeps going. After everyone in the group has had their 3 passes, rotate and switch players quickly and smoothly at the P2 and P3 positions so that those players get their turn.

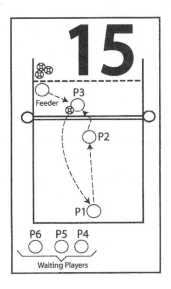

Emphasize:
Good quick lobs or throws right to the P1 position, good passes right to the setter (P2) position, and a smooth rotation and switching of players.
Run this drill:
Run it for only 15 minutes rapidly, then have the group move to the next station or a different drill.

The Zig Zag Passing Drill (No.16)
Object of the drill:
They learn to make passes rapidly then quickly move to a new position on the court.

What you will need:

You can use half the volleyball court with a net, and a coach with a cart of balls, and a whistle.

Working the drill:

Either demonstrate or remind your players how the drill is going to work, because it's tricky. Have players P1, P2, and P3 line up at the bottom of the court. The coach gets off to the side of the court with several balls. To start coach blows the whistle and lobs the ball up in the air to the middle of the court in front of P1. At the same time P2 and P3 sprint straight ahead to the middle of the court. P1 sprints under the ball and forearm passes to P2. As soon as P1 passes they break and sprint to P2's old location. P2 gets their pass and forearm passes the ball up in the air to P1. They get the pass then pass it up in the air to P3.

As soon as they pass, P2 breaks and sprints to P3's old location. P3 gets the pass and forearm passes it up in the air to P2 at their old location. After their second pass both P1 and P2 break and go to the end of the line. After P3 passes to P2 they break and go to the end of the line. P2 takes the ball then rolls it up to coach. After that, P4, P5, and P6 move up to the bottom of the court, and the whole process repeats. I suggest a walk through first so that everyone knows what to do.

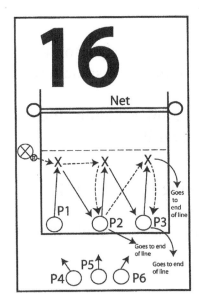

Emphasize: Good quick lobs and forearm passes up in the air, and players hustling to their next spot.
Run this drill: Run it for only 15 minutes rapidly, then have the group move to the next station or drill.

The Target Passing for Consistency Drill (No.17)
Object of the drill:
See how quickly and how many times players can hit the target square with the ball.
What you will need:
You will need a wall around the court someplace, and some colored tape to mark the squares on the wall.
Working the drill:
You could have maybe 3-6 squares marked on the wall. A suggestion is an 18 inch square. Have the players in the group line up about 8 feet away from the wall. You may need to adjust the distance away and height of the squares depending on the size of your team. On your whistle they toss the ball up in the air the try to pass it into the square.

You can have them use forearm or overhead passes. They need to pass it again before it hits the ground, over and over. They call the number of the pass out loud as they make it. They make 20 passes in a row then go to the end of the line. Have the player waiting their turn count the number of passes they get into the target square. The ball must hit inside the square, NOT an edge.

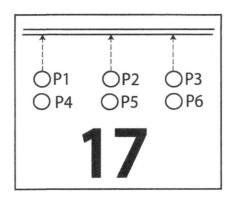

Emphasize: Good quick passes for accuracy.

Run this drill: Run it for only 30 minutes rapidly, then have the group move to the next station or a different drill.

The Slide Step Passing Drill (No.18)
Object of the drill:
They learn to control the direction of the pass.
What you will need:
You can use half the volleyball court and a cart of balls, and a whistle, or you can just go about anyplace inside or outside where there is some room to pass the ball around. The court works best though because you get the feel of a real game.
Working the drill:
You have 3 tossers P1, P2, and P3 up near the front row. P4 steps in the lower LH corner. On your whistle, P1 tosses the ball up in the air to P4. They immediately forearm pass the ball back to P1. Then they slide step to the right over to in front of P2. P2 tosses the ball up in the air to them, P1 passes it back, then slide steps over to in front of P3. P3 tosses the ball up in the air to P1. They immediately pass it right back. Then P1 slide steps to the left back to in front of P2, then the toss and pass backs repeat all the way back to P1. Then P4 goes to the end of the line. On your whistle, P5 steps up and the whole process starts over again.

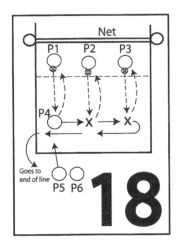

Emphasize:

Good quick tosses up in the air to the passer, and good passes up in the air back to the tosser, who is a simulated setter.

Run this drill:

Run it for only 15 minutes rapidly, then have the group move to the next station or a different drill.

Passing Skill Review

Common errors that need correcting

- Swinging of the arms.
- Bending the arms before putting the platform together (praying).
- Lifting up with the legs and body.

9. Individual Digging Techniques

The dig is sort of like the forearm pass except the movement has to be very quick. This is because this technique is an instantaneous response to receiving, then passing, a fast and hard to get to ball. There is a little time for movement in the forearm pass, but not the "dig." There are various corrections you can use to help your player become a better "digger." We will touch on these so you can help them by observing where their digs are going, compared to where they should have gone.

Skill Activity No. 56, 57- The Dig Technique

Object of the Drill:

Teach your players how to dig hard hit balls.

What you will Need:

You will need a full court with a net to work on, a bucket of balls, 2 coaches, and a whistle.

The Basics Are:

This is taking the forearm pass technique and altering it a little to become what is called a "dig". I suspect the technique got its name from watching a player go down real low with their hands, then sort of scooping or digging underneath the ball to keep it from hitting the floor. Teach your son or daughter to let the ball go as low as possible, which will give them just fractions of a second of more time to react. What they have to learn how to do is absorb the force of the ball by dropping the forearms down just as the ball makes contact. This is going to be hard for the little kids to learn. It will take lots of trial and error work with them to learn how to do this. Don't give up on them though because they can learn how to perform this technique. It's just going to take lots of patience on your part coach, mom, or dad, along with many repetitions. They should also flex and stiffen their elbows, and just flick the wrists, when the ball makes contact. At the same time their body needs dip way down low *(SEE FIGURE 56)*. This will make the ball get up in the air. Have them learn to direct the ball as close as possible to the front center of the court, in front of the net.

FIGURE 56

Working the Activity:
You can practice this technique out in the back yard, but the court is a better place. And you really do need a net to get the actual feeling of the ball coming hard over the top of the net though. Have them go any place in the back row and get into the "ready" position *(SEE FIGURE 26)*. When they see the ball is about to be hit, they put their thumbs together

in the forearm pass hands position *(SEE FIGURE 53)*. The next thing is, they have to step right at the ball with either foot *(SEE FIGURE 57-A)*. Which foot goes forward will depend on which side of them the ball is coming from. The next important thing to do is have them get their hips lower than the ball.

Teach them how to maneuver so that the ball comes down inside of their knees if possible. To work on this technique they are going to have to work on their quickness, agility, and flexibility drills. What they want to do is get the thumbs scooped under the ball just before contact. This way the ball will rebound off the wrists *(SEE FIGURE 57-B)*. They will have to learn to be careful making this move though, by flexing and pointing the thumbs down. If they point the thumbs up, the ball can hit on the end of the thumbs and possibly dislocate or injure them. This is especially true with the little kids and beginners.

When you get the hands and thumbs scooped under the ball, it will normally put back spin on it. However they must keep the hands and thumbs lower than the elbows so that the forearms are angled down *(SEE FIGURE 57-B)*. If the hands are even with, or higher than the elbows, then the ball can go up and over their head. We will talk more about this in the correction drill section next. The accuracy and direction of the "dig" is accomplished by pointing the thumbs in the direction you want the ball to go in.

Here is three training tips for you coach, mom, or dad. Number **one** _do not_ hit the ball too hard at the little kids and beginners. It really discourages them quickly. Number **two**, walk them through the body, feet, and hands position slowly until they catch on. Like step out and dip to the right, then to the left. Number **three**, let some air out of the ball for the little kids, so the hard hit balls don't sting so much on their forearms, or they can wear long sleeve shirts. They should practice this drill at least 3 times to the right, and 3 times to the left at a training session.

A   B
FIGURE 57

Emphasize:
Stress getting low and getting their hands under the ball
Run this drill:
Run it for only 15 minutes rapidly, then have the group move to the next station or a different drill.

Skill Activity No. 42- Dig Error and Corrections
The Basics are:
The reason I am adding this section in the drills is, I want you as coaches and parents to be able to correct their "dig" technique errors while they are trying to learn because this is going to be hard for the little kids. The technique is going to be very hard to teach young kids, and beginners, to perform successfully. So at least you will be able to watch them, and correct what they might be doing wrong. When the error is having the ball go straight up, or back over their head. The

correction is, don't hit the ball hard with their forearms. Stop the arms at contact and use a "poking" type move at the ball. Have them let the ball go down lower to the waist level, and keep their shelf (arms) angled down more in front.

When the ball comes off of their hands to low and won't go over the net.
The correction is, they have to get lower under the ball and scoop it more with the shelf (hands). To do this, have them go all the way down and touch the floor with their hands. Also have them bend the knees more, and keep their back straight as they go down for the ball. When the ball, hit to the center court position, does not get up in the air high enough (2 or 3 feet above the top of the net) for the setter; The correction is, have them flex and stiffen their arms, then just flick their wrists at the ball. All of these corrections will help them if you coach, mom, or dad, keep watching them while they are training. Then not to "harshly," but continuously, keep making the corrections with them. All the time while they are practicing their "dig" technique, keep watching and correcting them as necessary.

Team Digging Drills

Note:
Digging is offensively associated because after digging the ball has to get to a setter in an attempt to set someone up to score.

Partner Digging Drill (No.45)
Object of the drill:
Learn to make digs when the ball is at a players feet, or a little away to either side of them.
What you will need:
You will need half a volleyball court with a net, a cart with balls, a coach, a whistle, a feeder, and a passer.

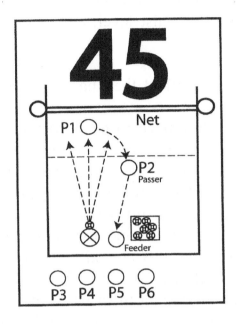

Working the drill:

This is going to be a tough drill for the younger kids. You may want to wait until they are 12 or older? Put a player P1 up in the front row, facing towards the backcourt. Coach stands facing them about 20 feet away, then overhand throws a ball directly at the feet of P1.

They need to get low and dig the ball over to P2, who passes to the feeder. The feeder always has a ball ready for coach, which keeps the drill moving. When P1 is comfortable digging straight at their feet then coach throws first to one side of P1 then the other. After about six throws, rotate and P3 steps up. After 12 throws rotate and switch the feeder and passer.

Emphasize:

Getting down low, and twisting the body to square up to throws to the side.

Run this drill:

Run the drill until each player gets their two cycles. After 30 minutes the group moves to the next station or a different drill.

The Dig and Cover Drill (No.46)
Object of the drill:

Learn to make digs when moving from back on defense then up to cover, then moving back to the back row.

What you will need:

You will need a volleyball court, a net, a cart with balls, a hitter/thrower, and a feeder.

Working the drill:

Have one player P4 go up by the net with a ball. Then have three players P1, P2, and P3 spread out in the back row. P4 hits or throws the ball hard at P1 (touch one), they dig it towards the feeder. Then they run up, touch the ten foot line and run back to where they were. Just as they get back P4 hits or throws another ball at them. They dig it toward the feeder (touch two), then run up touch the ten foot line, turn and go to the end of the line. Next P4 hits or throws to P2 and the drill repeats for two touches.

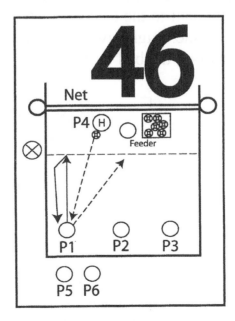

Then they hit to P3 and they repeat the drill for two touches. The feeder always has a ball ready for the hitter so that the drill keeps moving.

Emphasize:

Getting down low to dig and twisting their body to square up to throws to the side. Players need to hustle, so they get more digs in.

Run this drill:

Run the drill until each player gets at least four touches. After 30 minutes the group moves to the next station or start a different drill.

The Scramble Dive and Dig Save Drill (No.47)

Object of the drill:

This drill will be hard on the younger kids. You may want to wait until they have more experience, or they are 12 years or older.

What you will need:

You will need a volleyball court, a net, 2 carts with balls, a thrower, and a catcher.

Working the drill:

Coach takes a ball and goes up on the sideline near the front row. Then have player P1 step up into the back court. Coach tosses the ball up high in the air towards the middle of the front row. P1 sprints to the ball, dives, and digs the ball to the catcher, then rolls over, gets up, and goes to the end of the line. Right away P2 steps up, and the toss and dig repeats. Catcher tosses the ball in the cart.

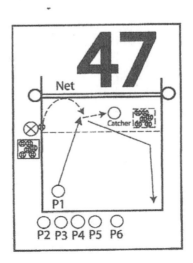

When coaches cart is empty, they switch carts. This keeps the drill moving. This drill wants to move fast for about 7 minutes. Then everyone rests for a few minutes, then the drill goes again.

Emphasize:

Getting to the ball quickly diving, and forearm digging the ball up in the air if possible to the catcher. Then executing the rollover and recover move, and getting up quickly. For safety purposes, make sure all your players have on elbow and knee pads for this drill.

Run this drill:

In 7 minute increments. After 30 minutes the group moves to the next station or starts a different drill.

The Teamwork Digging Drill (No.48)

Object of the drill:

Learn to make digs and use team work to get the ball back up to front court.

What you will need:

You will need a volleyball court, a net, a cart with balls, and a coach as a thrower.

Working the drill:

Coach gets a cart full of balls and goes up in the middle of the front row by the net. Then have three players P1, P2, and P3 spread out in the back row. Coach throws the ball hard at anyone of the players, they dig it towards one of the other players, who passes it back to the coach. Then they all go quickly back to their starting spot. Coach needs to mix up where they throw the ball, to make it harder for the players to dig the ball. After about 7 minutes rotate in three new players.

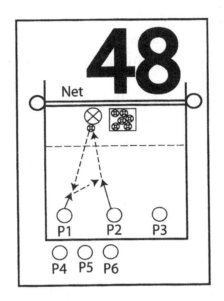

Emphasize:

Getting down low to dig, and getting a good dig up in the air that a teammate can get underneath to pass to coach.

Run this drill:

Run the drill until each player gets at least 3 minutes of work. After 30 minutes the group moves to the next station or starts a different drill.

10. Spiking and Hitting Techniques

Spiking and hitting ball over the net is very exiting to watch. The spike is a technique to hit the ball, over the net, very hard into the opponents side of the court. A full swinging arm motion is used to hit the ball as hard as possible. There are fundamentals skills though that kids have to learn, to be effective at spiking or hitting (sometimes called a kill). As an example, a good blocker can stop a spike. So you have to master all the techniques to be good at spiking. If the basic mechanics of the technique are not followed correctly, the ball can go out of bounds, or into the net. This is going to be hard for kids, that can't reach the top of the net, to learn. You may have to wait until they are 12 years old or more, to work on this technique.

Some coaches say start teaching young kids and beginners to spike the ball at about 15 feet back from the net. Then gradually work with them closer, and closer, to the net as they begin to master the technique. Along with the technique, there are four different footwork movement approaches *(SEE PAGES 12 THRU 15)*. In this section we will only go through the techniques of spiking and hitting, not the approach footwork.

Skill Activity No. 39- The Hard Driven Spike and Arm Swing Technique
Object of the Drill:
Teach your players how to make the arm swing for a hard driven spike.
What you will Need:
You will need a full court with a net to work on, 2 coaches, and a whistle.

The Basics Are:
There seem to be at least two slightly different six step techniques for the spike arm swing. The one we will use is a little easier for young kids. The teaching technique is, have your son or daughter go through each step kind of animated. That is one at a time slowly, holding momentarily at each one. This is again "muscle memory." Then when they master each step, they put it all together in one arm swing movement. These steps can be practiced without the ball. Add the ball to the training after they master the six steps. This type of spike usually comes from the side of the court. For left handed spikers everything is just flip flopped or opposite. The 6 steps are as follows:

A   B   C   D

E   F

FIGURE 39

1. For right handed swingers, have them stand up with the right foot slightly forward. Knees just slightly bent. Both arms up in front with the elbows bent at 90 degrees to the ground. The hands facing each other in a kind of praying position *(SEE FIGURE 39-A)*.

2. Bend at the knees and step back with the foot so that the leg is almost parallel to the ground. Drop both arms so that the hands are pointing down at the ground *(SEE FIGURE 39-B)*.

3. Step forward with one leg. Swing the hitting arm back so that it is almost parallel to the ground. Bring the other arm up and straight out at the side for balance. Both knees are slightly bent in a crouch position *(SEE FIGURE 39-C)*.

4. Start to push off on the toes for the jump up. Bring one foot up along side the other. The hitting arm is still back, but the elbow is bent in behind the head. The wrist is cocked back ready to make the hit on the ball. The other hand up and forward a little, still slightly outward for balance. This drops the shoulder down just a little *(SEE FIGURE 39-D)*.

5. Now they are jumping up. The body rotates slightly to the hitting side. Both legs straighten out, and the hitting leg goes back to get the proper swing momentum. The hitting arm is still back, but the elbow goes from behind the head to the forearm pointing slightly up. The wrist stays cocked for the hit on the ball. The back arches, the other arm straightens out and points up at about 45 degrees for the down swing momentum *(SEE FIGURE 39-E)*.

6. While up in the air the hitting arm swings around hard making the hit on the ball, with the base of the palm contacting the bottom third of the ball. At contact, the hand rotates over the top of the ball and then rolls on over so that the fingers are pointing down at the ground. This puts top spin on the ball, and makes it drop quickly to the floor. Simultaneously the other arm starts to swings down to get the necessary   momentum for the hitting arm swing *(SEE FIGURE 39-F)*.

Working the Activity:
To practice the "hard driven spike" you coach, mom, or dad, will need to find a court with a net. You can set up a net in your back yard, or find one at a court someplace. If your son or daughter is really serious about playing volleyball, it might be a good idea to buy one, and set it up in the back yard. Once you have discussed the 6 steps of the arm swing with them, call out the numbers "one," "two," etc., and have them go through each step.

They should walk through the whole sequence at least 2 times. Have them start out about 15 feet back from the net, then give them the ball and let them go through all 6 steps at full speed, and spike a ball over the net. They should go through the full speed arm swing sequence at least 3 times at a training session.

Emphasize;
The right hand position and getting a hard hit on the ball.

Run this drill:
Run the drill until each player gets their two cycles. After 15 minutes the group moves to the next station or a different drill.

Skill Activity No. 40- The Off Speed Spike

Object of the Drill:
Teach your players how to make the off speed spike.

What you will need:
You will need a full court with a net to work on, 2 coaches, and a whistle.

The Basics are:
The off speed spike is a slightly different type of spike. This is a technique to fool the opponent into thinking you are going to make the hard hit spike right at them. The object of this type of spike is to make the hit into an open space on the court. This type of spike has to look just like the hard driven spike, except the player slows the arm, and the wrist snap, at the last minute of the jump up. And instead hits the ball with the palm of the hand. The player may take a full swing at the ball,

56

but then eases up and makes a soft hit into an open area on the opponent's side of the court. The arm swing would be the same as in *FIGURE 39,* except the hit is with the palm of the hand.

Working the Activity:

Practice this the same as in Drill No. 39, except show them how to hold their hand, so that they hit the ball with their palm *(SEE FIGURE 40)*. They should go through the whole arm swing sequence at least 3 times at a training session. They can walk through this two times at first if they need to.

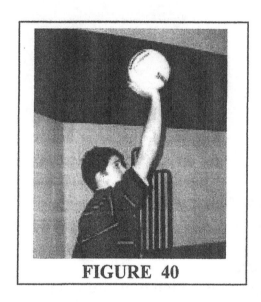

FIGURE 40

Emphasize;

Holding their hand just right so that they hit the ball with their palm.

Run this drill:

Run the drill until each player gets at least 3 hits. After 15 minutes the group moves to the next station or a different drill.

Skill Activity No. 41- The Standing Spike Technique

Object of the Drill:

Teach your players how to make the standing spike.

FIGURE 41

What you will Need:

You will need a full court with a net to work on, 2 coaches, and a whistle.

The Basics are:

The standing spike is kind of a "I don't have time to" move. It would be when the player does not have time to make an approach or a jump. Some coaches call this a "down ball." It's called by this name because the player just reaches up and hits the ball straight down to the floor, from a standing position ***(SEE FIGURE 41)***. This is going to be hard for kids, that can't reach the top of the net, to learn. You may have to wait until they are 12 years old or more, to work on this technique.

Working the Activity:

To practice the "standing spike," coach you, mom, or dad, will need to find a court with a net. You can set up a net in your back yard if you have one, or find one at a court someplace. You need a net, so you make sure they get the ball over it while practicing. Have them stand 1 or 2 feet in front of the net, then lob or throw the ball to them several feet over their head. What they have to do is, turn slightly to either side so they see the ball coming to them. Next, just as the ball starts to come down at a point just a little above the top of the net, they stretch up on their toes. Then they reach up and kind of push the ball down on the other side of the net using their fingers. They should do at least 2 of these. First turning to one side then turning to the other side and do 2 more. This will make them more versatile at the net.

There are also several lead-in drills, and games, that can be used by parents to help improve on their spiking skills. There are quite a few of these drills and games to go over so what we will do is pick out some of the better ones to use. See further on in the book in the "Games" section

Emphasize;
The right hand position then quickly going up and getting a hard hit on the ball.

Run this drill:
Run the drill until each player gets at least their 4 hits. After 15 minutes the group moves to the next station or a different drill.

Skill Activity No. 43- The Kneeling Spike with a Partner Technique
Object of the Drill:
Teach your players how to make their spikes by hitting down on the ball.

What you will Need:
You will need half a court with a net to work on, 2 coaches, a whistle, and a shagger to chase the balls.

The Basics are:
This is a drill to sharpen their skills for hitting the ball down, and hard. A partner or helper holds the ball with both hands way out in front of their body. The player kneels down on the floor or ground, just to the side of the partner holding the ball *(SEE FIGURE 43)*. Then the player makes a spike type hit on the ball. By rotating their wrist over the top of the ball, they get top spin on the ball which makes it drop or move

downward *(SEE FIGURE 39)*. You coach, mom, or dad, or a partner (friend) needs to hold the ball high enough up in the air so that it is about a little higher up than their forehead.

Working the Activity:

To practice this drill you can go out to the back yard or the court. Have them get down on their knees, then you coach, mom, dad, or a friend, take the ball and get just to the side of them. Hold the ball out on your finger tips so they can hit the ball, and not your hands. Then have them hit the ball, instructing them to hit it with the palm of their hand making contact on the lower third of the ball first. Tell them to make sure the fingers then roll over the top of the ball as they make the hit. They should make at least 3 hits from each side at each training session.

FIGURE 43

Emphasize;

The right hand position then hitting down on the ball.

Run this drill:

Run the drill until each player gets at least their 6 hits. After 15 minutes the group moves to the next station or a different drill.

Team Spiking Drills

These are drills you can run with the whole team involved. You keep running these drills every once in a while to sharpen up the footwork of all your players.

The Three Part Footwork Drill (No.301)

Object of the drill: Learn the basic footwork steps for the take off.

What you will need: You will need a volleyball court, a net, a coach with a cart of balls, and a shagger.

Working the drill: Demonstrate to your players how each step works. Explain to them that this is a three part progression drill. Start by having two players move up to near the front row, to save on time. Players shag their own ball, bring it back to coach and go to the end of the line. Rotate players and make sure each one gets two spikes for each of the three take offs.

PART 1. STANDING IN PLACE

Coach sets to P1. They take one step with the left foot from a standing position, make their arm swing and spike the ball over the net. Coach immediately sets P2. They take one step and spike the ball over the net. Let each player have two spikes then they become the shagger.

PART 2. TWO STEPS AND HIT

Coach sets to P1. They take two steps from a standing position, make their arm swing and spike the ball over the net. Coach immediately sets P2. They take two steps and spike the ball over the net. Let each player have two spikes then they become the shagger.

PART 3. THREE STEPS AND HIT

Coach sets to P1. They take three steps from a standing position, make their arm swing and spike the ball over the net. Coach immediately sets P2. They take three steps and spike the ball over the net. Let each player have two spikes then they become the shagger.

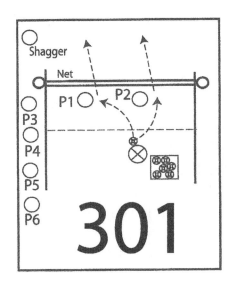

Emphasize:

Tell the players to make sure they hit the bottom third of the ball, snap over the top, and use the correct footwork steps.

Run this drill:

Run drill until all player get at least two spikes at each progression.

The Pop Up With Arms Only Drill (No.302)

Object of the drill:

Learn the correct arm movement during approach without using a ball.

What you will need:

You will need a volleyball court with a net.

Working the drill:

Demonstrate to your players how their arms are going to move in their approach to the hit. Start by having two players move up to near the front row, to save on time. If you have the little kids, you might try three in the front row to save time. To help, tell them to visualize a downhill skier with ski poles in their hands. On first step; they dig poles in the snow in front of their body. On the second and third steps; they push their body down the hill while throwing their arms back as they plant to make their jump. Next both arms go up in the air as they jump. Due to an opposite foot plant, the hitting arm shoulder should be back. If your players are having trouble, have them try walking through all the moves first. Players make two pop ups with arm swings, then go to the end of the line. Rotate players and make sure each one gets two pop up swings.

Emphasize;

Working on just coordinating their arm swings and steps with their jump.

Run this drill:

Run drill until all players get at least four "pop ups." Run the drill for 15 minutes then move on to a different drill or station.

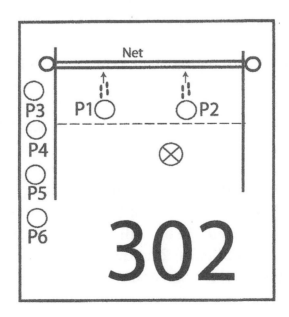

The Hitting Arm Swing Only Drill (No.303)
Object of the drill:
Learn the correct arm swinging movement during the approach, without using a ball (see Drill 302 diagram).
What you will need:
You will need a volleyball court with a net.
Working the drill:
Demonstrate to your players how their arm swings and shoulders are going to move as they make the hit. Start by having two players move up to near the front row, to save on time (see Drill 302 diagram). If you have the little kids, you might try three in the front row to save time, and get in more swings

Both arms are high at the end of the approach. The hitting shoulder is back, The opposite arm needs to drop down as the hitting arm comes through the swing. Then they swing through an imaginary ball. Basically this is dry run training for muscle memory. Players make two pop up swing through hits, then go to the end of the line. Rotate players and make sure each one gets two arm swing through hits.

Emphasize:
Working on coordinating their arm swing through with their shoulder back and opposite arm drop.
Run this drill: Run drill until all players get at least four" arm swing through hits." Run the drill for 15 minutes then rotate players to a different drill or station.

The Kneeling Spike Drill (No.304)
Object of the drill: Learn to hit the ball down on their spikes.
What you will need: You will need a volleyball court with a net, a coach with a cart of balls, 2 holders, and maybe a shagger.
Working the drill: Demonstrate to your players how rotating their wrist over the top of the ball gives it top spin on the ball causing it to drop or move downward. Each player will need a partner for this drill. The hitting player gets down on one knee or both knees, whichever is more

comfortable for them. I suggest using a folded towel under their knee(s). The partner stands in front and just to the side of the hitter, and on the same side as the spiking hand.

They hold the ball in their finger tips, with arm outstretched in such a way that the hitter will not hit the holders hands when they swing. On the coaches whistle, have each player make three hits on the ball, then both players switch and the holder becomes the hitter. If your players are having trouble, have them try walking through all the hand ,wrist, and finger moves first. When both players make their three spike hits, then they go to the end of the line. Rotate players and make sure each pair of partners gets their three spike hits. A shagger can chase the ball. Coach keeps tossing the holder a ball, to keep the drill moving.

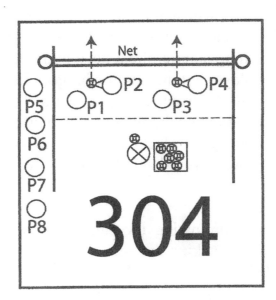

Emphasize:
The palm of their hand making contact on the lower third of the ball first, and the fingers rolling over the top of the ball as they make the hit.

Run this drill:

Run drill until all players get at least three kneeling hits on the ball. After 30 minutes they move to the next station or start a different drill.

The Criss Cross Hitting Drill (No.305)

Object of the drill:

Hitters learn to criss cross in the front row for confusion to blockers, with only one making the hit.

What you will need:

You will need a volleyball court, a net, a coach with a cart of balls, a setter, and a shagger on the other side.

Working the drill:

Demonstrate to your players how they are to criss cross with only one making the hit. Players can have a signal to each other so that they know which one will make the hit. The one making the hit can signal the other hitter and setter using just about anything the opposition won't notice, something simple like a head nod, adjusting their knee pads, or fingers. The player not making the hit goes in front, makes a fake swing, and screens out the front row opponent's. The hitter makes their hit go across court and bounce to the out side. Hitters go to the end of the line, two new hitters get in place. The setter makes a set right in the middle of the front row. Coach has a ball ready for the setter to keep the drill moving.

Emphasize:

Working on coordinating the timing on the criss cross run, and the signal on who is making the hit.

Run this drill:

Run drill until all player get at least two spikes. After 20 minutes or so the group moves to the next station or starts a new drill.

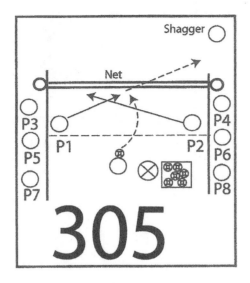

The Back Court Hitting Drill (No.33)

Object of the drill:

Hitters learn to make longer hits from the back row.

What you will need:

You will need a volleyball court, a net, a cart of balls, a setter, and a shagger on the other side of the net.

Working the drill:

Demonstrate to your players how they are to make the hit from the back court. Coach lobs a ball up in the air to the setter in the very back center of the court. Setter makes a set first to P1 position then the P2 position. The hitters (P1 or P2) make a hit on the ball from back court, then go to the end of the line. P4 and P5 position players move up to P1 and P2. P6 and P7 move to the P4 and P5 positions. After every player has had one turn, rotate a new player to be the setter. Coach always has a ball ready to lob to the setter, which keeps the drill moving.

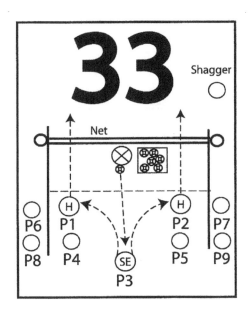

Emphasize;

Getting a good solid hit from back court that makes it over the net, but does not go out of bounds.

Run this drill:

Run drill until all players get at least three hits from back court. After 30 minutes the group moves to the next station or start a new drill.

The Pick the Hit Attack Drill (No.34)

Object of the drill:

Hitters learn to make different types of hits from the front row around a blocker.

What you will need:

You will need a volleyball court, a net, a cart of balls, a feeder, a setter, a shagger, and blocker on the other side.

Working the drill:

Demonstrate to your players how they are to make the hit from the coaches signal. Coach stands behind the blocker and just to the side to signal the shot they want. This way the blocker has no idea of what's coming. The shot options are a roll hit, an off speed hit, a tip in hit, or just a regular hard jam spike. Coach can use a special signal or hold up fingers. The signal is given just before the hitter starts to make their jump. P1, P2, and P3 work the drill for three hits, then rotate all three players. You can also rotate the blocker if you like.

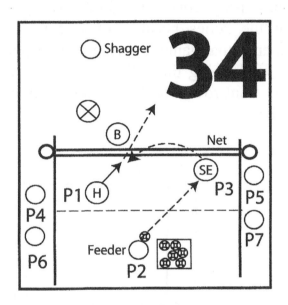

Emphasize:
A high jump up, and executing the hit called for.
Run this drill:
Run the drill until all players get at least three hits. After 30 minutes the group moves to the next station or starts a new drill.

The Target Hitting Drill (No.35)
Object of the drill:
Hitters learn to make their hits go to a specific part of the court.
What you will need:
You will need a volleyball court, a net, a coach with a cart of balls, a setter, a feeder, and a shagger on the other side of the net.

Working the drill:

Demonstrate to your players how they are to make the hit to a specific part of the court. Coach stands in the middle of the backcourt, and signals the hitter where they want the hit to go, just as the hitter starts to run up for the hit. In fact coach can do the feeding to the setter, to get more players involved in the hitting. Divide the other side of the court into six zones using cones. I would have your players get used to numbers for the zones because opponents won't know where that number is in an actual game if they hear it, especially the younger kids. Coach starts by lobbing the ball to the setter, who makes a set to the middle of the front row. The hitter comes up and makes the hit to the zone called for.

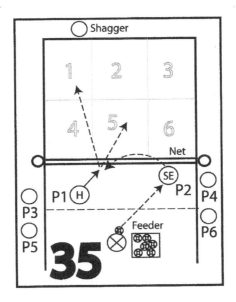

Emphasize:

Making a high jump up, and executing the hit to the zone called for.

Run this drill:

Run the drill until all players get at least three hits. After 30 minutes the group moves to the next station or starts a new drill.

11. Tipping Techniques

The "tip" is sort of like a fake hard spike. It is an off speed technique where the jump up looks like a straight hard spike, but the ball goes just over or around the blocker(s). The idea is to fool the opponent.

Skill Activity No. 59- The Tip Technique
Object of the Drill:
Teach your players how to fake a hard swing and just tip the ball.
What you will Need:
You will need a full court with a net to work on, 2 coaches, a whistle, a stand in blocker, and a shagger to chase the balls.
The Basics are:
The approach and arm swing is the same as the "spike" *(SEE FIGURE 39-A THRU D)*. Contact with the ball is made with the finger tips of the hitting hand, and not on the base of the palm of the hand. The point of contact should be just below the center back of the ball so that the ball goes just up and over the outstretched hands of the blocker(s) and falls quickly to the floor behind the blocker *(SEE FIGURE 59)*.

FIGURE 59

If there is a single blocker, who is tall and gets way up in the air, you can twist the hand and wrist, to direct the ball just around the side of the blockers arm on either side of them.

Working the activity:
To practice this you will need a net and a court. Or you could go out to the back yard with a net. Practice this technique the same way as with "the spike", except they stop the arm and lock the elbow just before the contact is made. Probably the best thing to do is, walk them through the arm and hand action before trying it at full speed. What you can do coach, mom, or dad, is have them stand back just a foot or so behind the net, and face the net. Then next you stand beside them with the ball, and toss it just above their head and between them and the net. As you toss it up, they extend their hitting hand and use a flicking pushing type action with their out stretched fingers to get the ball just over the top of the net.

If the ball goes into the net when they try to tip it, the ball is probably too far away from their front hitting shoulder. Also the lower the ball drops before contact, the more likely it will go into the net. Have them work on their timing with the "set" to improve their skills for this technique. When they have mastered the hand movements of the technique, then have them go back about 3 or 4 steps away from the net and go through the whole approach, jump up, arm swing, and fake spike.

What you want to show and teach them how to do is learn how to grimace the face, and use the eyes to really sell the blocker that you intend to spike the ball hard. Some kids will naturally catch on to the technique of making a good fake, and others will not. Keep working with them on this because they can learn how to do it. This should not be practiced by young kids and beginners until they are 12 years old or over. When they have mastered the technique, they should make at least 3 of these tips at a training session.

Emphasize;
Working on their finger tips for tipping the ball.
Run this drill:
Run the drill until all players get at least three tips. After 15 minutes the group moves to the next station or starts a new drill.

Team Tipping Drills

These are drills you can run with the whole team involved. You keep running these drills every once in a while to sharpen up the tipping skills of all your players.

The Tipping Drill (No.36)
Object of the drill:
Learn the basic technique of the tip hit.
What you will need:
You will need a volleyball court with a net, a cart of balls, 2 coaches, a whistle, a setter, a feeder, and a shagger on the other side of the net.
Working the drill:
Demonstrate to your players how they are to make the tip over the blockers outstretched arms and fingers. Feeder stands in the middle of the backcourt, starts by lobbing the ball to the setter, who makes a set to the middle of the front row. The hitter comes up and makes the tip. Coach can stand just behind the blocker, and signal which side to make the tip towards.

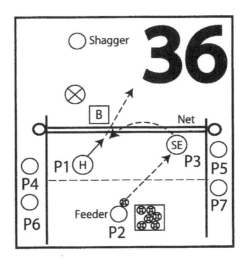

Emphasize;

Making a good high jump up, and executing the tip by keeping the arm stiff instead of swinging it on down.

Run this drill:

Until all players get at least three tips. Rotate P2 and P3 after 9 tips. After 30 minutes the group moves to the next station.

The Tooling a Block Drill (No.37)

Object of the drill:

Learn the basic technique of hitting the ball off a blockers outside arm (use Drill 36 diagram).

What you will need:

You will need a volleyball court, a net, a cart of balls, 2 coaches, a whistle, a setter, a feeder, a blocker, and a shagger on the other side of the net.

Working the drill:

This works the same as Drill 36 except the hit is made off the blockers outside arm. The hitter comes up, checks as they go up where the outside of the blockers arm is located, then hits the ball right off the blockers outside arm, going down and away to the outside.

Emphasize;

Making a high jump up, and executing the hit by aiming for the blockers outside arm.

Run this drill: Run the drill until all players get at least three consecutive hits. Rotate and switch P2, P3, after 9 hits. After 30 minutes the group moves to the next station or starts a new drill.

The Roll Off a Block Drill (No.38)

Object of the drill:

Learn the basic technique of hitting the ball off a blockers out stretched hand and fingers (use Drill 36 diagram).

What you will need:

You will need a volleyball court, a net, a cart of balls, 2 coaches, a whistle, a setter, a feeder, a blocker, and a shagger on the other side of the net.

Working the drill:

This also works the same as drill 36, except the hit is made off the blockers inside hand and fingers (RH hitters), then rolled away and down. Demonstrate to your players how to roll the ball off the blockers inside hand, then down and away

Emphasize:

Making a high jump up, and executing the roll off down and away to the inside of the blocker. This is because they usually expect you to go outside.

Run this drill:

Run the drill until all players get at least three consecutive roll off hits. Rotate and switch P2, P3, after 9 tips. After 30 minutes the group moves to the next station or start a different drill.

Spiking and Tipping Skill Review
Common errors that need correcting

- Using backwards footwork
- Not using the arms in the approach.
- Planting square instead of having opposite foot forward.

12. Setting and Overhead Passing Techniques

Setting and overhead passing are very important fundamentals your players need to learn. This is a basic skill to direct the ball towards another team mate, or set up a attacker for a spike. As a pass, it is probably the most accurate. Setting is a technique for getting the ball to a spiker, high enough above the net for the spiker, so they can hit the ball into the opponents side of the court. The player that sets the ball up for an attacking spiker is called a "setter." The overhead pass can be used to accomplish several things. It can be used to receive a serve. It can be used to direct the ball to the setter. Or it can be used to hit the ball directly over the net to the opponents side of the court. The overhead pass is probably harder for young kids to learn than the forearm pass. This is because it takes strong fingers and wrists to control the ball correctly. Explain to your players that the overhead pass should be used when the ball is coming in at shoulder height or higher, and with not to much force.

A setter has to determine which player is in the best position to make an attack or spike. The setter is usually the player in the middle of the front row. This is because from this central position they can set the ball in several directions. This is a basic fundamental technique that all players should work on very hard to perfect. We will go over the basic skill first then some drills to help perfect the technique.

Skill Activity No. 306, 307- The Basic Overhead Pass Technique
Object of the Drill:
Teach your players how to make their passes for setting the ball.

What you will Need:
You will need half a court to work on, 2 coaches, a whistle, and maybe a shagger to chase the balls.

The Basics are:

The overhead pass is basically for balls that are up in the air and moving slowly. When used properly the overhead pass is the most efficient pass to use in handling the ball. Tell your players not to use this technique though unless the ball is coming in shoulder height or higher. The first thing to teach them is the ready position *(SEE FIGURE 306)*. To be ready for the pass, the feet should be about shoulder width apart, right foot slightly forward, hands cupped and raised just above the forehead. The knees are slightly bent in a crouch position, the body leaning just a little forward so their weight is on the balls of their feet.

FIGURE 306

The hands should be shaped like the volleyball with the thumbs in *(SEE FIGURE 307-A)*. The eyes are set to look for the ball between the thumbs and fingers. The wrists are slightly cocked back and the fingers spread. The hands are relaxed and placed about 6 inches out in front of the forehead. The ball should be contacted just above the head, and on the pads of the fingers *(SEE FIGURE 307-B)*. The passer should know where, and who, they want to pass the ball to before the ball gets to them. Just before the ball gets there, they should square their shoulders toward the player they intend to pass the ball to. As the ball contacts their fingers, they extend the arms and legs upward using a little flicking type action with the wrists and fingers *(SEE FIGURE 307-C)*.

Working the activity:

To practice this pass coach, mom, or dad, you can go out to the back yard, driveway, or on the court. All you will need is a little room. With the real little kids, start out at about 3 or 4 yards away from each other. Lob the ball up in the air to them at first until they catch on to the technique. Later on you can forearm, or overhead, the pass to them to make it more like a game situation for them. When the ball comes in to them, have them overhead pass the ball back to you. They should make about 13 of these passes back to you at a session. Watch them carefully, and make sure they are using their wrists and fingers properly.

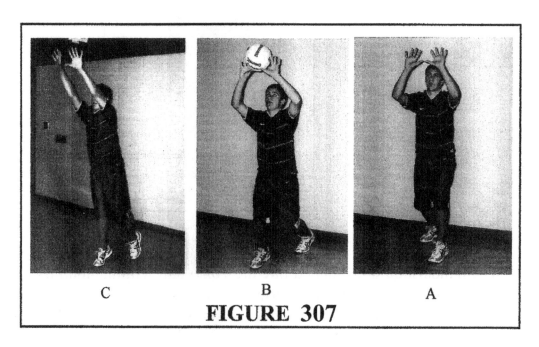

C   B   A

FIGURE 307

Emphasize;
They use their fingers and wrists correctly.

Run this drill:
Make sure players each get a least 3 overhead passes at a practice session. After 30 minutes move them to a different drill.

Skill Activity No. 308, 309- Setting the Ball Technique

Object of the Drill:
Teach your players how to correctly set the ball to a teammate.

What you will Need:
You will need half a court to work on, 2 coaches, a whistle, and maybe a shagger to chase the balls.

The Basics are:
Setting the ball is another technique that uses the overhead pass. The "setter" receives a pass from a team mate, then makes a "*high outside set*" overhead pass, above the net, for the attacker or spiker to hit. The setter is usually in the middle of the front row, but not always. Sometimes a back row player can make a "*quick set*" overhead pass up to the front row for the attacker or spiker to hit. There is another type of set where the setter makes a "*back set*" overhead pass behind them to a attacker or spiker *(SEE FIGURE 308)*.

To make the "*high outside set*" (most common), the setter turns, usually to the side, leap hop steps, then makes the set. When the ball gets to them, just above the head, they make a high looping overhead pass that comes down right in front of the net next to the side line.

To make a "*quick set*", the setter leap hops, then makes the set. The pass can come from the back row or the front row. When the ball gets to them, just above the head, they make a quick lower overhead pass only a few feet above the net, to a front row attacker or spiker.

To make a "*back set*", the setter leap hops, then makes the set. When the ball gets to them, just above the head, they make an over the head, behind them pass, to the attacker or spiker. Just as the ball starts to make contact with the fingers, they have to crouch down at the knees, arch their back, and roll their wrists back, in order to get the ball to go behind them *(SEE FIGURE 309)*. This will probably be too hard for the real little kids. You may have to wait until they are 12 years old or more, to work on this technique.

FIGURE 308

FIGURE 309

Working the activity:

To practice the "set" passes coach, mom, or dad, you will need to find a court with a net. You can set up a net in your back yard, or find one at a court someplace. If your player is really serious about playing volleyball over the long term, it might be a good idea to buy a net, and set it up in the back yard if you have the room

To practice the "*high outside set,*" have them stand right at the middle of the net, and back away from it several feet. You may need a helper, mom or dad, to work on this drill at home. One to stand back and lob the ball to them, then you mom or dad stand out to the edge of the net to catch their "set" pass. When the ball gets to them, they have to make a high outside overhead pass to the edge of the net *(SEE FIGURE 308)*. Also by standing out there you can observe their technique, to make sure they do it correctly. They should do at least 2 of each of these sets, to each side of them, at each training session.

To practice the "*quick set,*" have them first stand right at the middle of the net, and back away from it several feet. You may need a helper, mom or dad, to work on this drill at home also. The helper can stand back and lob the ball to them, then you mom or dad stand about 1 or 2 yards away from them, to either side of the net to catch their quick low "set" pass. When the ball gets to them, they have to make a short two foot up in the air overhead pass *(SEE FIGURE 308*. As you stand there simulating a spiker, observe that their set only goes a few feet above the net. Also check to see the rest of their movements are correct. Another version of this drill is, have them stand at all the positions in the back row, then have the helper lob the ball to them. Then you, mom or dad, stand in the front row at different places. They have to quick set" the ball to you as you simulate the spiker. Make sure they get it to you quickly, and at just a few feet above the net. They should do at least 2 of these sets, to each side of them, at each training session.

To practice the "*back set,*" have them first stand right at the middle of the net, and back away from it several feet. You may need a helper, mom or dad, to work on this drill at home also. The helper can stand back and lob the ball to them, then you mom or dad stand out near the edge of the net behind them, to simulate the spiker and catch their "set" pass. When the ball gets to them, they have to make an, over their head and behind them, outside pass to the edge of the net *(SEE FIGURE 309)*. Also by standing there you can observe their technique to make sure they make the pass over their head correctly. This pass should be higher than the quick set pass, but lower than the high outside pass *(SEE FIGURE 308)*.

Emphasize;
They work on getting all 3 of their sets exactly where they need to go.

Run this drill:
Make sure each of your players get a least 2 sets at all three positions at a practice session. After 30 minutes move them to a different drill or station.

Skill Activity No. 310- Learning The Finger Control Technique
Object of the Drill:
Teach your players how to correctly use their fingers to control their overhead pass ball sets

What you will Need:
You will need a wall to work on, 1 coaches, a whistle,

The Basics are:
This is a drill that teaches them to overhead pass the ball using the fingers. It is basically standing in front of a wall, and overhead passing, or kind of dribbling the ball back and forth from the fingers to the wall. The object is to only use the fingers to push the ball to the wall *(SEE FIGURE 310)*.

Working the activity:
To practice this training technique you will have to find an large wall to work on. Have them stand about 3 feet in front of the wall. Next they hold the ball, with both hands, right in front of their forehead. Keep the

hands flat and the thumbs in. Then they just push the ball against the wall using only the fingers. The ball will bounce quickly back, so they have to keep using their fingers to keep it going back and forth against the wall (dribbling). They want to keep it bouncing, without dropping it, if possible. They should do this drill for at least 3 minutes at a training session.

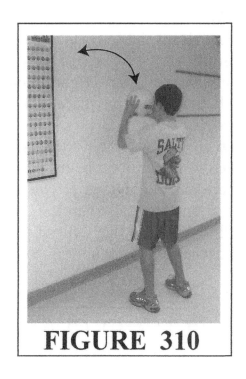

FIGURE 310

Emphasize:
Keeping the ball bouncing against the wall by just using their fingers.
Run this drill:
Make sure each of your setters get a least 3 minutes of bouncing the ball against the wall at a practice session. After 15 minutes move them to a different drill or station.

Team Setting and Overhead Passing Drills

These are drills you can run with the whole team involved. You keep running these drills every once in a while to sharpen up the setting and overhead passing skills of all your players.

The Setting Ready Position Drill (No.19)

Object of the drill:
Learn to get the hands up and ready to make the set.

What you will need:
You can use the volleyball court, right up close to the net in the center position is best, but just about anyplace with a little room will work.

Working the drill:
Have your group all get in a row if there is room. Demonstrate to them on how and when to get into the ready position for the set. Have them all just stand there relaxed looking at you then stand back a few yards and say, "Ready," and they all snap to a ready position, hold it there until you say, "Relax," then they all put their arms down. Have them rest a few minutes then say it again.

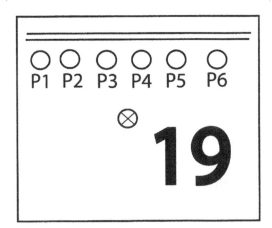

Emphasize;
Both hands up just above the top of their head, palms flat facing out, fingers spread, and thumbs almost touching

Run this drill:
Run it for about 15 minutes then have the group move to the next station or a different drill.

The Center Setting Position Drill (No. 20)
Object of the drill: Learn to make three different sets from the center position.
What you will need: Use a volleyball court, right up close to the net in the center position is best, a cart of balls, a coach, a whistle, possibly a shagger, and a basket of balls.
Working the drill: There are three variations to this drill.
- The quick set.
- The High Outside set.
- The Back set.

Demonstrate to your players on how and where to make each one of these sets. Coach needs to be sure and make nice high lobs to the setters so that they can get under the ball.

   1. The Quick Set.
      Have them make a short two foot or so higher than the net, and next to the edge, overhead pass set. P2 can catch the set and roll the ball back to coach.
   2. The High Outside Set.
      Have them make a high overhead pass set to P2 over near the edge of the court. P2 can catch the set and roll it back to coach.
   3. The Back Set.
      Have them make a medium height overhead type pass back over their head to P3. Demonstrate to them how to bend over backwards to do this. P2 can catch the set and roll the ball back to coach.

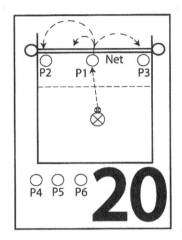

Emphasize:

Hands up just above the top of their head, palms flat facing out, fingers spread, and thumbs almost touching, to make their overhead catch and set. Also have them work on facing and squaring their hips to the target of the set, and making the set at just the right height.

Run this drill:

Let each player have two tries at each of the three sets, then rotate and switch players. Run the drill for 30 minutes then move to another station or drill.

The Outside Setting Position Drill (No.21)

Object of the drill:

They learn to get the hands up and be ready to make the set from either outside position.

What you will need:

Use a volleyball court, right up close to the net in either one of the outside positions is best, a coach, a whistle, a cart of balls, and a shagger. Use two balls, alternating, to keep the drill moving rapidly.

Working the drill:

Have P1, P2, P3 all get in the front row. Demonstrate to them on how and where to make the sets. There are two sets to work on.

1. *The High Middle Set.*

Have P2, then P3 make a high overhead pass set to P1 near the middle edge of the net. P1 can catch the set and roll it back to coach.

2. *The Quick Set.*

Have P2, then P3 make a short quick set overhead pass to P1 moving over near the edge of the net. P1 can catch the set and roll it back to coach.

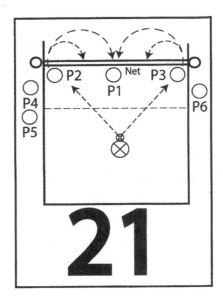

Emphasize;

Hands up just above the top of their head, palms flat facing out, fingers spread, and thumbs almost touching. Also have them make sure they face and square their hips to the target of the set.

Run this drill:

Let each player have ay least two tries at each of the sets. Run the drill for 15 minutes then rotate and switch players.

The Wall Drill (No.22)
Object of the drill:
Learn to use the correct footwork, and arm and hands position.
What you will need:
You will need a wall, some tape, and each player needs a ball.

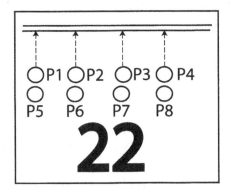

Working the drill:
Put 6 one foot long strips of tape on the wall, spaced going up at one foot apart at different heights on the wall, depending on how big your players are. You could maybe start at a 5 foot height and go up. Do this 4 places across the wall at maybe 8 feet apart. Put a player with a ball at each set of tapes, about 4 feet out from the wall.

On your whistle they all step out left-right with their feet, and overhead set the ball hitting the bottom tape strip first then working their way up with one after the other "catch-set-catch-set" and so on for 10 times, calling out their number each time. The idea is get REPS. They can rest a minute or two between sets then do another 10.
Emphasize;
Left-and then Right with feet, hands up, using the fingers, and calling out their number of sets.

Run this drill:

Run it for only 30 minutes then they move to the next station or drill activity. If you have more players than wall spots, then rotate and switch players after every set of 10.

The Set and Fake Drill (No.23)

Object of the drill:

Learn to make a nice high set where one player fakes a spike, and the other player tips it in the other direction

What you will need:

You will need a court with a net, a coach with a cart of balls, a whistle, and a shagger near the net.

Working the drill: There are two variations of this drill. One from a center set, and one from an outside set.

1. CENTER SET (SEE 23-A)

Coach lobs the ball up in the air to P1 in the center position. They make a real high set just a little to their right. At the same time P3 runs over fast from the right side, and fake swings a spike going to the left. Also at the same time P2 starts to come over to the center court. They let P3 swing through their fake, then they pretend to make a left handed tip going to the right. The idea is to confuse potential blockers on the other side of the net.

2. OUTSIDE SET-RIGHT OR LEFT (SEE 23-B)

Coach lobs the ball up in the air to P1 in the left outside position. They make a real high set to the center of the net. At the same time P3 runs over fast from the right side, and fakes swings a spike going to their left. Also at the same time P2 lets P3 clear in front of them, then they move up and fake a little tip or dink to the right side. The idea here is the same, confuse the blockers.

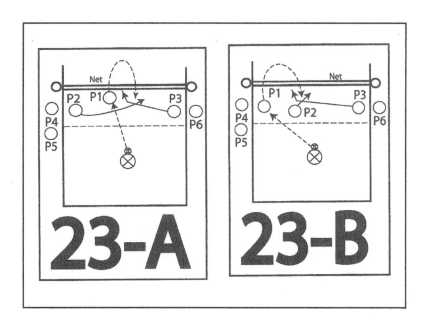

Emphasize;

The fakes for this drill because this practice is for the setter to get the set at the right height. The key for the fake spike and tip in is the timing. It has to be practiced to get it just right.

Run this drill:

Let each player have two tries at 23-A, then switch and rotate the players. Let each player have two tries at 23-B, then switch and rotate players. Run it for only 30 minutes then they move to the next station or drill activity.

The Footwork Drills (No.311)

Object of the drill:

Learn to get the setter's footwork down.

What you will need:

You will need a court with a net, a cart of balls, a coach, a whistle.

Working the drill:

There are four variations of this drill. One the perfect pass, two backing up, three is four-steps off, and four is two-steps off.

1. PERFECT PASS
Setter doesn't have to move to get to the ball. Coach makes a perfect lob pass up in the air to them, just a little bit in front of them.

2. BACKING UP
Setter has to back up using back stepping. Coach makes the lob pass just a little behind them so that they need to back up.

3. FOUR-STEPS OFF
Setter needs to make four shuffle steps forward to get under the ball. Coach makes the lob pass about four steps out in front of the setter.

4. TWO-STEPS OFF
Setter needs to make two shuffle steps forward to get under the ball. Coach makes the lob pass about two steps out in front of the setter.

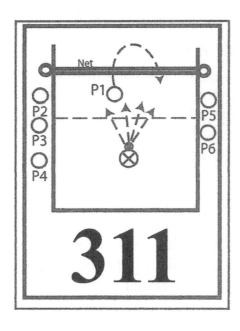

311

Emphasize;
Making the correct footwork moves for each of the four toss lobs.
Run this drill:
Let each player have one try at each of the four moves, then switch and rotate players. Have players get quickly into position so that the drill runs rapidly and smoothly. Run it for only 30 minutes then they move to the next station or drill activity.

The Rapid Sequence Setting Drill (No.312)
Object of the drill:
Learn to make rapid sets one after the other, which builds muscle memory.
What you will need:
You will need a court with a net, a coach with a cart of balls, and a feeder. Or rotating players can act as a feeder to keep the drill moving quickly.
Working the drill:
There are four setting variations of this drill. One the high middle set, two the high outside set, three the quick middle set, and four the high back set.

1. HIGH MIDDLE SET
Setter moves to a spot just a little off center front court, then makes a high set to the right center of the front row. Coach needs to make a perfect high lob toss just a little in front of P1.

2. HIGH OUTSIDE SET
Setter stays in slightly off center front court position, then makes a high outside set to the right. Coach needs to make a perfect high lob toss just a little in front of P1.

3. QUICK MIDDLE SET
Setter stays in slightly off center front court position, then makes a quick lower set to the right. Coach needs to make a perfect high lob toss just a little in front of P1.

4. HIGH BACK SET

Setter stays in slightly off center front court position, then makes a high back set behind them. Coach needs to make a perfect lob toss just a little in front of P1.

Emphasize;

Coach calls the type of set to be made, then makes a perfect high lob toss just a little in front of the setter. Feeder needs to quickly hand coach a ball. Setter needs to work on getting just the right height to each of the sets.

Run this drill:

Let each player have one try at each set rapidly one after the other going to the right, then they flip-flop positions, move slightly right, and rapidly set four times to the to the left. Then switch and rotate players. Run the drill for only 30 minutes or slightly longer if necessary so that each player gets a turn, then they move to the next station or drill activity.

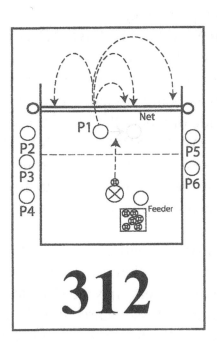

The Read The Blocker Drill (No.313)

Object of the drill:

Learn to see and read what the blockers are doing on the other side of the net.

What you will need:

You will need a court with a net, a tosser with a cart of balls, and a feeder. Rotating players can act as a feeder to keep the drill moving quickly.

Working the drill:

There are three setting variations of this drill. One the coach is on the opposite side of the net from a center setter, two a player blocker is on the side opposite the center setter, and three the coach is on the opposite side of the net, and the setter is coming to center net from the back row.

1. CENTER SET WITH COACH

Tosser lobs a throw to the setter in the front row center (313-A). Coach holds up two fingers, a clip board, or some other visible object. P1 must look and call out what the coach is holding up before setting the ball.

2. CENTER SET WITH A BLOCKER

Tosser lobs a throw to the setter in the front row center (313-B). A middle blocker starts in middle then moves outside to outside just as the ball is being tossed. P1 must look, then set the ball to the opposite side of where the blocker is moving.

3. BACK ROW TO FRONT CENTER SET WITH COACH

Tosser makes a throw towards front center front row (313-A). P1 moves from back row position to front center, and calls out what the coach is holding up before setting the ball.

Emphasize;

Coach needs to occasionally get closer to the net making it harder for the setter to see what they are doing while setting from the center position. Tell your setters they need to learn how to take a very quick glance just before the tosser starts to make their throw. The feeders need to very quickly give the tosser the next ball to keep the drill going.

Run this drill:

Let each player have at least one try at each of the three variations, then quickly switch and rotate players. Make sure players get quickly into position so that the drill runs rapidly and smoothly. Run it for only 30 minutes then they move to the next station or drill activity.

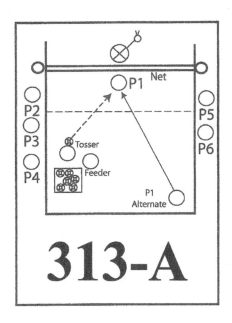

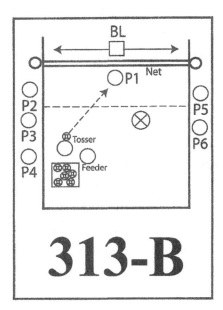

The Player Setting Drill (No.314)

Object of the drill:

Learn to make continuous moving sets with four players.

What you will need:

You will need a court with a net, a coach with cart of balls, and maybe a shagger. Coach has a ball ready in case a set gets away. If it gets away the players let it go to keep drill going.

Working the drill:

All four players get involved in the sets. If a player can not make a set because of a bad lob to them, they catch the ball and toss it up to the next player to keep the drill going. To start coach blows a whistle and lobs the ball to P1, who forward sets the ball to P2, they forward set the ball to P3, who forward sets the ball back to P1, they backward set the ball to P4, who forward sets the ball back to P3, who again forward set back to P1. They roll the ball back towards the ball cart. It might be a good idea to have a shagger back by the ball cart. Coach blows a whistle to end the set. Switch and rotate players after one round of sets. P1 is out new player is in. The rest of the players rotate clockwise to new position. To make the drill harder for older experienced players, have them move backwards to the line of the set so that they are moving into the ball when they make their sets.

Emphasize;

Players must use their hands to catch the ball so they don't get into the habit of forearm passing the ball. Have them work on making good high sets.

Run this drill:

Let each player have at least one try at each of the four positions, then quickly switch and rotate players. Make sure players get quickly into position so that the drill runs rapidly and smoothly. Coach needs to grab another ball and have it ready to keep drill running fast. Run it for only 30 minutes then the group moves to the next station or drill activity.

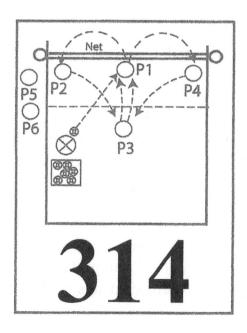

314

Setting Skill Review
Common errors that need correcting
- Thumbs are pointing outward.
- Flicking wrist on the extension.
- Hands are uneven.
- Feet are even and no extension.
- No leg extension.

13. Serving the Ball Techniques

Serving is the technique that puts the ball in play during a match. The ball is served from behind the end line *(SEE DIAGRAM 1)*. The rules say the ball must be tossed up or released by the server, then struck or hit with one hand. The object of the serve is to start play by getting the ball over into the opponents side of the court. An excellent serve is called an "ace" when the opponent can not return the ball back to the servers side of the court after it goes over the net. An ace is also a quick way to score points during the match. There are 5 basic fundamental types of techniques for serving the ball. There is the "side float serve", the "underhand serve", the "overhand float serve", the "roundhouse serve," and last the "jump serve."

The "underhand" serve is probably the most common technique for the real little kids to learn first. The "jump" serve is probably the most difficult to learn. I would suggest waiting until they are 12 years old or more before attempting to teach them the "jump" serve technique. One more thing to mention is, some of the better youth volleyball coaches say, teach the little kids to get the hip moving forward with the arm. This is what puts some power into the serve. In this section we will cover all the basic fundamental techniques, and some lead-in drills to improve on their skills.

Skill Activity No. 44- The Underhand Serve Technique

Object of the Drill:

Teach your players how to make the underhand serve.

What you will need:

You will need a full court with a net to work on, 2 coaches, a whistle, and a cart of balls..

The Basics Are:

This is probably the easiest and best basic serve for the real little beginning kids to learn. It's also easier to control because it does not involve a toss up in the air. Since right handed serve players are more common, we will use the right hand for the explanations. A left handed serve would flip flopped or just the opposite on movements. First have them put the left foot forward. Their weight should be shifted so it is on the right (back) foot. The left hand is forward, stretched out, palm up, with the ball supported on the pads of the fingers. The right arm is all the way back with the palm down *(SEE FIGURE 44-A)*.

The next step is to hit the ball. As the arm swings forward to hit the ball, the weight is shifted to the left (front) foot. As the right arm begins it's swing forward, the ball is dropped down out of the left hand. The right hand swings immediately on forward, making contact with the ball on heel of the open hand. The right arm follows through towards the top of the net. The eyes should be on the ball, and the right arm and leg should be in line with the follow through as the arm swings on through *(SEE FIGURE 44-B)*.

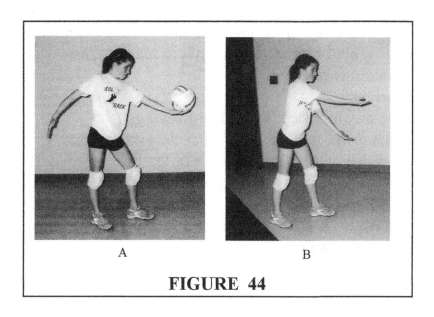

A   B

FIGURE 44

Working the activity

To practice the "underhand serve," you will have to have a net. You can practice in your back yard with a net, but it's better to find a court someplace. Have them stand at the back of the court, behind the end line. For the real young kids and beginners, walk them through all the movements without the ball first. Then when you see they understand the technique, you can give them the ball and let them make some serves. If you see the ball is going too high in the air and not getting over the net, they are probably holding the ball wrong. Have them hold the ball at waist level or lower. Also make sure they are contacting the ball just below the back center part of the ball.

When the ball does not make it over the net, it's probably because the server is swinging their holding hand. Make sure they keep the holding hand still, and they are making contact with heel of an opened hand. Also they will get more power to hit the ball if they rotate their hips forward with the swing. If your player is standing behind the end line watching the ball after serving, tell them to get in the habit of moving up into the back of the court immediately after swinging the arm. This is so they will be up in the court, in a defensive position, just in case there is a quick hard hit return. Have them make at least 3 of these serves, at each training session.

Emphasize;
Making the right steps and the arm swing.
Run this drill:
Run the drill until all players get at least three serves. After 30 minutes the group moves to the next station or starts a new drill.

Skill Activity No. 315- The Side Float Serve Technique
Object of the Drill:
Teach your players how to make the side float serve.
What you will need:
You will need a full court with a net to work on, 2 coaches, a whistle, and a cart of balls..
The Basics Are:
This is the second easiest serve for the real young beginning kids to learn. Because it is a side arm motion though, it does tend to go out of control out of bounds many times. The side spin action does have some advantages though. It makes it harder to get the ball up in the air for a good "set" on the return from the opposing team. Again we will use the right hand for the explanations. For a left hand player the movements are just the opposite.

Start by having them put their left foot forward with the toes facing to their right toward the side line *(SEE FIGURE 45-A)*. The left leg is directly back behind the right front leg, at about shoulder width apart, with the toes pointed towards the right side line. The left hand is pointed to the right side line, about chest high, holding the ball with the palm up supporting it on the pads of the fingers. The right hand is extended back ready to make the hit. A short step is taken with the left foot as the right arm is brought back. The palm is facing forward with the fingers

100

slightly bent in a half fist. The weight is on the right (front) foot *(SEE FIGURE 315-A)*.

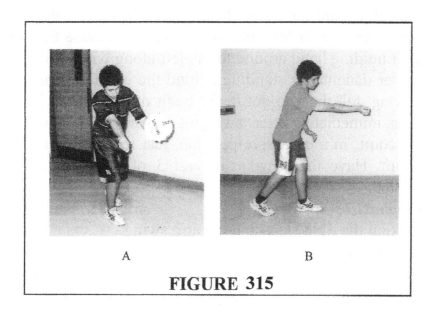

FIGURE 315

The next step is to hit the ball. As the arm swings forward to hit the ball, the weight is shifted to the left (front) foot. As the right arm begins it's swing forward, the ball is dropped down out of the left hand. The right hand swings immediately on forward, making contact in the center of the ball with the heel or base of the palm. As the arm swings forward the hips have to turn and push forward along with the arm swing. The right arm follows right through the center of the ball, with the palm pointing towards the top of the net. The eyes should be on the ball, all the way through the follow through *(SEE FIGURE 315-B)*.

Working the activity:

To practice the "side float serve," you will have to have a net. You can practice in your back yard with a net, but it's better to find a court someplace. Have them stand at the back of the court, behind the end line. For the real young kids and beginners, walk them through all the movements without the ball first. Then when you see they understand the technique, you can give them the ball and let them make some serves. If you see the ball is going too low in the air, and not getting over the net, they are probably holding the ball wrong. Have them hold the ball a little higher at chest level. When the ball goes out of bounds way over to their left side, it's probably because the server is swinging their holding hand around to the left along with their arm swing. If your son or daughter is standing behind the end line watching the ball after serving, tell them to get in the habit of moving up into the back of the court immediately after swinging the arm. This is so they will be up in the court, in a defensive position, just in case there is a quick hard hit return. Have them make at least 3 of these serves, at each training session.

Emphasize;
Making the right steps and the arm swing.

Run this drill:
Run the drill until all players get at least three serves. After 30 minutes the group moves to the next station or starts a new drill.

Skill Activity No. 316, 317- The Overhand Float Serve Technique
Object of the Drill:
Teach your players how to make the overhand float serve.

What you will Need:
You will need a full court with a net to work on, 2 coaches, a whistle, and a cart of balls.

The Basics Are:
This is a very basic fundamental serve for 12 year olds and up. It is a harder faster serve than the side float or the underhand serve. It can be hard to return by the other team because the trajectory is low and more flat. This can be a very accurate serve technique if it is performed correctly. The problem usually for beginners is the toss up. It has to be just right for the hit to be accurate and straight. Younger kids can start working on this technique though by starting out at 10 to 15 feet from the net. Then working back farther and farther towards the end line as

they begin to master the technique. This technique also takes a little more strength than some of the other serves. So have them work on strengthening their arms and legs. Again we will use the right hand for the explanations. For a left hand player the movements are just the opposite.

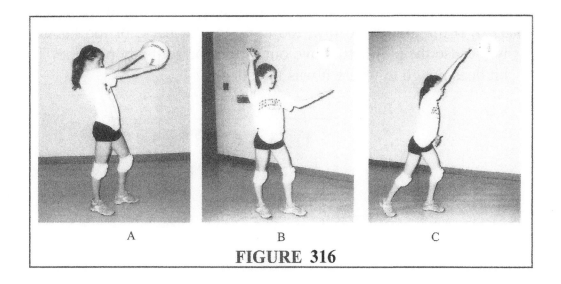

A   B   C

FIGURE 316

Start by having then stand with the shoulders facing toward the net. The left foot is slightly in front. Both arms are holding the ball straight out in front. Their weight is evenly distributed between both feet *(SEE FIGURE 316-A)*. Next they take a step forward with the left foot. Toss the ball up *(SEE FIGURE 317)*, bring the right arm back, elbow up high and back, and the hand behind the right ear. The fingers are spread, the hand is flat, and the palm is facing forward. The eyes are on the ball *(SEE FIGURE 316-B)*. Immediately the right arm and hand swing forward while keeping the eyes on the ball. Contact with the ball is made on the center back part of the ball, with the heel part of the open hand. Use a poking action upon contact with the ball, but no follow through. Just stop the hand after the hit. The weight is shifted to the left (front) foot *(SEE FIGURE 316-C)*.

The overhand serve toss can be tricky. In the standing position with the right arm back, the left arm lifts up the ball 12 to 18 inches above the extended left hand. The toss has to be straight up right in front of the left shoulder. Think of the ball just like an extension of the left hand as it goes up. The toss is the key to this whole technique *(SEE FIGURE 317)*. If the toss is too low, too high, too far back, or too far in front it will cause the player to move out of the correct body position. Then the hit does not go to where it was intended.

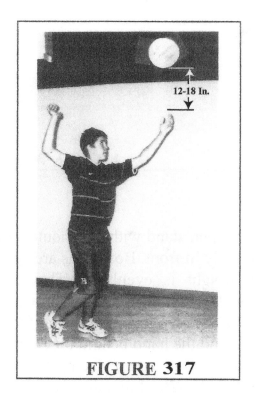

12-18 In.

FIGURE 317

Working the activity:
To practice the "overhand float serve," you will have to have a net. You can practice in your back yard with a net, but it's better to find a court someplace. Before they start, have them practice just the toss by itself.

Have them first work on the arm movement without the ball. When you see they are catching on to correct arm movement, then add the ball. The key here is just a quick little lift up with the arm, while keeping the body kind of still until the ball leaves the hand. Again, many repetitions translates to "muscle memory."

Have the real little kids and beginners start out about 10 feet back of the net if they are going to try this. They should make their serves in slow motion at first. Then speed it up little by little. When they can get the ball over the net then have them move back several feet at a time until they are back behind the end line. Also mom or dad, watch and make sure they are poking the ball, and not making a big arm swing slam type of hit on it. If your son or daughter is standing behind the end line watching the ball after serving, tell them to get in the habit of moving up into the back of the court immediately after swinging the arm. This is so they will be up in the court, in a defensive position, just in case there is a quick hard hit return. Have them make at least 10 of these serves, at each training session until they can get it over the net from behind the end line. Then they only need to make 5 serves at a session.

Emphasize;
Making just the right lift up with the ball and the correct arm swing.
Run this drill:
Run the drill until all players get 5-10 serves. After 30 minutes the group moves to the next station or starts a new drill.

Skill Activity No. 318, 319- The Roundhouse Serve Technique
Object of the Drill:
Teach your players how to make the roundhouse serve.
What you will need:
You will need a full court with a net to work on, 2 coaches, a whistle, and a cart of balls.
The Basics are:
The roundhouse serve is not too common. However, it is one of the basic techniques being used. This type of serve will be hard for kids to

learn, especially the real little kids. The arm swing is a little unnatural for most kids. There is an advantage to this serve. You can generate more power than you can with the underhand serve. It also takes more skill because it involves making a toss with the ball. Again we will use the right hand for the explanations. For a left hand player the movements are just the opposite. Start by having them stand, turn and face the right side line. The feet are about shoulder width apart. The left foot is forward with the toes pointing to the right net post. The right serving hand is straight back, palm up, about waist high.

The left hand is forward directly in front of the left shoulder, stretched out about waist high, palm up, with the ball supported on the pads of the fingers. The knees are just slightly bent *(SEE FIGURE 318-A)*. The next step is to hit the ball. The ball is then tossed straight up in the air and just above the head about 12 to 18 inches. And as with all toss ups the eyes have to keep focused on the ball all the way to contact. The right arm then immediately swings around and over the head, making contact with the ball right in front of the body near the top of the toss. All during the forward swing, the arms have to remain extended. As the arm is swinging, the weight is shifted to the left (front) foot.

The hips have to rotate forward, followed by the right shoulder. The left shoulder dips down and the left arm along with it. The right foot is lifted up on the toes by the swinging movement. This could be described as a windmill type motion with the arms *(SEE FIGURE 318-B)*. Contact with the ball is made with the heel of the open hand, just below the center back part of the ball. The hand should kind of poke the ball, without any follow through. In other words the hand just stops after the hit is made. The left leg provides balance so that the server does not fall over forward *(SEE FIGURE 318-C)*.

A   B   C

FIGURE 318

The roundhouse serve toss can be tricky. In the standing position with the right arm back, the left arm lifts up the ball 12 to 18 inches above the head. The toss has to be straight up right in front of the left shoulder. Think of the ball just like an extension of the left hand as it goes up. The toss is the key to this whole technique *(SEE FIGURE 319)*. If the toss is too low, too high, too far back, or too far in front it will cause the player to move out of the correct body position. Then the hit does not go to where it was intended.

FIGURE 319

Working the activity:

To practice the "roundhouse serve," you will have to have a net. You can practice in your back yard with a net, but it's better to find a court someplace. Before they start, have them practice just the toss by itself. Have them first work on the arm movements without the ball. When you see they are catching on to correct arm movement, then add the ball. The key here is just a quick little lift up with the arm, while keeping the body kind of still until the ball leaves the hand. Again many repetitions translates to "muscle memory." Have the real little kids and beginners start out about 10 feet back of the net if they want to try this. They should make their serves in slow motion at first.

Then speed it up little by little. When they can get the ball over the net then have them move back several feet at a time until they are back behind the end line. Also coach, mom, or dad, watch and make sure they are poking the ball, and not making a big arm swing slam type of hit on it. If your player is standing behind the end line watching the ball after serving, tell them to get in the habit of moving up into the back of the court immediately after swinging the arm. This is so they will be up in the court, in a defensive position, just in case there is a quick hard hit return. Have them make at least 10 of these serves, at each training session until they can get it over the net from behind the end line. Then they only need to make 5 serves at a session.

Emphasize;
Making just the right lift up with the ball and the correct arm swing.

Run this activity:
Run the drill until all players get 5-10 serves. After 30 minutes the group moves to the next station or starts a different drill.

Skill Activity No. 50- The Jump Serve Technique

Object of the Drill:
Teach your players how to make the jump serve.

What you will need:
You will need a full court with a net to work on, 2 coaches, a whistle, and a cart of balls.

The Basics are:
The jump serve is probably the hardest of all the serves to perform. The jump has to be just right, and the toss has to just right in order for the technique to work properly. Because it is similar to the "spike," it is very exiting for fans   to watch. And for that reason many young kids want to learn how to do it. The jump adds power to the serve which makes it more difficult for the other team to return. This is probably the fastest and the hardest serve, but it is always difficult to know where it's headed. The toss is really the key to this serve. Without a good toss it's direction is very unpredictable.

Again we will use the right hand for the explanations. For a left hand player the movements are just the opposite. Start by having them stand, shoulders facing the net, and the left foot slightly forward. The weight should be on the back foot. Both hands are extended forward, holding the ball, at about shoulder height, with the right hand on the top of the ball *(SEE FIGURE 50-A)*.

Next they are going to take a 3 step approach. Step out with the left foot first. After the *first step* they will toss the ball up, using the right hand. Use the fingers to put forward spin on the ball. The toss should be up in the air in front of the left shoulder, and forward out about 2 steps ahead of them. This is because when they take the other 2 steps, the ball will be right where they want it and not behind them. They should keep their eyes on the ball all the way until they make the hit on it. I suspect the height of the toss will have to be at least 2 feet above their extended hand height when they jump. It will probably take some trial and error practice to get the toss up height just right *(SEE FIGURE 50-B)*.

The second step should be with the right foot as they move toward the ball. The arms should move back in preparation for the jump *(SEE FIGURE 50-C)*. Step forward with the third step, and plant the left foot as the hands start to come forward *(SEE FIGURE 50-D)*. Start the jump up by rotating the right shoulder back. At the same time bring the right arm back, raise the elbow up high, with the hand back behind the head. Then reach upward for the ball *(SEE FIGURE 50-E)*. Make contact on the bottom of the ball, while it's at it's highest point.

Lock the elbow, and use the base of the palm. At contact rotate the wrist, with a little snap forward, at a 90 degree angle. This should put top spin on the ball. Last follow through with the right arm. This is one of two different ways to make contact with the ball. The other way is, make contact with the ball on the center back part of the ball. Use more of a poking action, with an open hand and hardly any follow through. I suspect the first way is better though because it puts spin on the ball. The spin makes it harder for the opponents team to make a return of the serve *(SEE FIGURE 50-F)*.

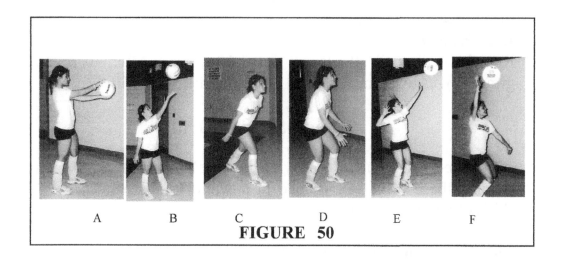

A B C D E F

FIGURE 50

Working the activity:

Have the real little kids and beginners start out about 10 feet back of the net if they want to try this. They should make their serves in slow motion at first. Then speed it up little by little. When they can get the ball over the net, then have them move back several feet at a time until they are eventually back behind the end line. Also coach, mom, or dad, watch and make sure they are contacting the ball correctly, and not hitting it any old way. If your player is standing behind the end line watching the ball after serving, tell them to get in the habit of moving up into the back of the court immediately after swinging the arm and making the hit.

This is so they will be up in the court, in a defensive position, just in case there is a quick hard hit return. When they are serving from behind the end line it's ok if they land in the court after the jump. However, they have to make the hit on the ball while in the air, then land in the court. Have them make at least 10 of these serves, at each training session until they can get it over the net from behind the end line. Then they only need to make 5 serves at a session.

Emphasize;

Making just the right lift up timing with the ball, the correct jump, and the correct arm swing.

Run this drill:

Run the drill until all players get 5-10 serves. After 30 minutes the group moves to the next station or starts a different drill.

Team Serving Drills

These are drills you can run with the whole team involved. You keep running these drills every once in a while to sharpen up the serving skills of all your players.

The Basic Ball Serving Drill (No.1)

Object of the drill:

Learn the basic serving techniques.

What you will need:

You will need a net, a court, 2 coaches, a whistle, and a cart of balls. If you have a backyard net, use some cones to mark the end line spacing from the net.

Working the drill:

Youth team serving basically means getting the ball over the net. Even if it's not pretty, tell them it's very important that they get the ball over the net every time or it's a turnover. For the younger kids it's really going to depend on how much skill they have. First have them use the technique that's easiest for them. Maybe it's not the serve you would rather have them do, but which one they can do best until they get a little older and with more experience. Explain to them about staying behind the line. Show them how the ball is held for the underhand and overhand serves. Demonstrate how the arm swing works for each of these techniques. Then have them try it, but without the ball. If they are having trouble, then have them go through the arm swing in slow motion until they get it right.

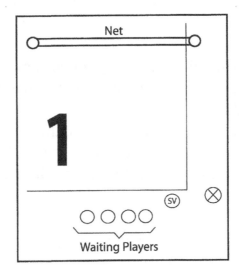

Emphasize;

Holding the ball still, getting a good arm swing, and not going over the line.

Run this drill:

Have them try each technique 2 times, then let the next player try. Run all the way through the group once, or stop in 30 minutes then move on to the next station.

The Underhand Serve Technique Drill (No.2)

Object of the drill:

Learn the basic technique of underhand serving. This is the easiest serve for beginners to start out learning.

What you will need:

You will need a net, a court, 2 coaches, a whistle, and a cart of balls. If you have a backyard net, use some cones to mark the end line spacing from the net.

Working the drill:

Have your players in the group come up one at a time to try the serve. Briefly demonstrate how to hold the ball, the arm swing, and the hand position required. Have them focus on a spot slightly above the net to aim their swing. Until they get older have them just aim for the center of the far court.

Emphasize;

Holding the ball still, getting a good arm swing, not going over the line, and hitting the ball hard enough to get it over the net every time.

Run this drill:

Have them try the technique 2 times, then let the next player try. Have a ball ready for the next player. Stop the drill after 30 minutes and have the group move to the next station or a different drill.

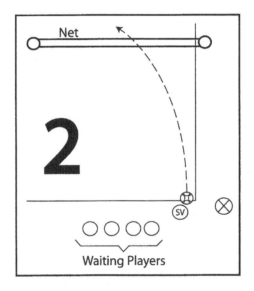

The Side Float Serve Drill (No.3)

Object of the drill:

Learn the basic technique of side float serving. This is the second easiest serve to learn (refer to Drill No. 2 picture).

What you will need:

You will need a net, a court, 2 coaches, a whistle, and a cart of balls. If you have a backyard net, use some cones to mark the end line spacing from the net.

Working the drill:

Have your players in the group come up one at a time to try the serve. Briefly demonstrate how to hold the ball, the arm swing, and the hand position required. Have them focus on a spot slightly above the net to aim their swing. Until they are older have them just aim for the center of the far court.

Emphasize;

Holding the ball still, getting a good arm swing, not going over the line, and hitting the ball hard enough to get it over the net every time. Have them really concentrate and focus with their eyes on the ball, and the center spot on the far court, all the way through the arm swing and follow through.

Run this drill:

Have them try the technique 2 times, then let the next player try. Have a ball ready for the next player. Stop the drill after 30 minutes and have the group move to the next station.

The Overhand Float Serve Drill (No.4)

Object of the drill:

Learn the basic technique of the overhand float serve. This is the basic technique for 12 year olds and up. (SEE FIGURE 316 on Pg. 103)

What you will need:

You will need a net, a court, 2 coaches, a whistle, and a cart of balls. If you have a backyard net, use some cones to mark the end line spacing from the net.

Working the drill:

Have your players in the group come up one at a time to try the serve. Briefly demonstrate how to hold the ball, the arm swing, and the hand position required. Have them focus on a spot slightly above the net to aim their swing. Until they older have them just aim for the center of the far court.

Emphasize;

Holding the ball still, getting a good arm swing, not going over the line, and hitting the ball hard enough to get it over the net every time. Have them really concentrate and focus with their eyes on the ball, all the way through the arm swing and follow through. Also they need to work on getting a consistent toss up height.

Run this drill:

Have them try the technique 2 times, then let the next player try. Have a ball ready for the next player to keep the drill moving. Stop the drill after 30 minutes and have the group move to the next station or a different drill.

The Jump Serve Drill (No.5)

Object of the drill:

Learn the basic technique of overhand jump serving (refer to Drill No.2 picture). This is the basic technique for the older experienced players.

What you will need:

You will need a net, a court, 2 coaches, a whistle, and a cart of balls. If you have a backyard net, use some cones to mark the end line spacing from the net.

Working the drill:

Have your players in the group come up one at a time to try the serve. Briefly demonstrate how to hold the ball, the arm swing, and the hand position required. Have them focus on a spot slightly above the net to aim their swing. Until they older have them just aim for the center of the far court.

Emphasize:

Holding the ball still, getting a good arm swing, not going over the line, and hitting the ball hard enough to get it over the net every time. Have them really concentrate and focus on their run up and jump, the ball, and their take off point and getting height, which will actually take them out over the end line and into the court while in the air. Tell them to expect lots of practice because this technique is very difficult to learn and execute.

Run this drill:

Have them try the technique 2 times, then let the next player try. Have a ball ready for the next player to keep the drill moving. Stop the drill after 30 minutes and have the group move to the next station or a different drill..

The Roundhouse Serve Drill (No.6)

Object of the drill:

Learn the basic technique of roundhouse serving (refer to Drill No.2 picture). This technique is not to often used, but it can work for some players.

What you will need:

You will need a net, a court, 2 coaches, a whistle, and a cart of balls. If you have a backyard net, use some cones to mark the end line spacing from the net.

Working the drill:

Have your players in the group come up one at a time to try the serve. Briefly demonstrate how to hold the ball, the arm swing from in back, and hand position required. Tell them to expect lots of practice because this technique is also more difficult to learn and execute.

Emphasize;

Getting a good toss up, the roundhouse type arm swing, not going over the line, then hitting the ball hard enough to get it over the net every time. Have them really concentrate and focus with their eyes on the line, then the ball all the way through the toss up, arm swing, and follow through, or they might miss contact at just the right spot on the ball. Tell them to expect lots of practice because this technique is more difficult to learn and execute.

Run this drill:

Have them try the technique 2 times then let the next player try. Have a ball ready for the next player to keep the drill moving. Stop the drill after 30 minutes and have the group move to the next station or a different drill.

Serving Body Mechanics Drill (No.7)

Object of the drill:

To improve body mechanics during the serve motion.

What you will need:

You will need a wall to throw against, 2 coaches, a whistle, and a cart of balls.

Working the drill:

Have your players each stand in front of a wall, or a feed back net, in a row about 5-6 feet away. They put a ball in their serving hand up near their ear. Next they step out with the opposite foot while shifting their hips forward and throwing the ball against wall or net. Tell them to try and throw it harder each time. This should make them shift their weight automatically. Their rear foot stays anchored to the ground.

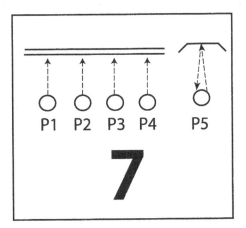

Emphasize;

Using good footwork, then making a hard throw with their back foot anchored.

Run this drill:

Blow your whistle and have them each try the technique 3 times, rest a few minutes, then blow your whistle for 3 more tries. Run this activity for at least 30 minutes then move on to the next station.

Tossing Skill Activity (No.8)

Object of the drill:

Learn to toss the ball out in front of the them to get more consistent serving toss up accuracy.

What you will need:

You will need a cart of balls, 2 coaches, a whistle, two long sticks or broom sticks, and some space out around the court someplace, or even out in the backyard.

Working the drill:

Put two intersecting sticks down on the ground or court. Have the players in the group come up one at a time, and stand out about 2 feet in front of the sticks intersection. They take the ball, toss it up just a little over head height, and try to get it to land consistently at the stick intersection in front of their hitting hand. Briefly demonstrate how to do it, then let each player come up and make 2 tries then go to the end of the line. They must also step out with their non hitting side foot and shift their hips.

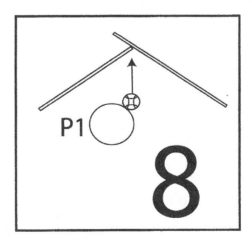

Emphasize:

The mechanics of a consistent toss up arm swing, along with the step out.

Run this activity:

Blow your whistle and have them each try the technique 2 times with everyone getting a turn, then go to the end of the line. Run this activity for at least 30 minutes then move on to the next station or a different drill.

Serving Skill Review
Common errors that need correcting
- Inconsistent tosses will cause most of the errors.
- Lifting back leg causing loss of balance.
- Not shifting weight to get hips in front of shoulders.
- Closing contact hand.

14. Offensive Plays and Group Tactics

There are a number of offensive plays, individual tactics, and group tactics that your players need to know. These are the plays and tactics they need to know and execute when they are on offense. My first bit of advice is don't worry about what the opponent's can or can't do. Have your players only worry about what they need to do. This section breaks down into "individual" and "group or team" tactics. Individual tactics are coordinated offensive actions a player needs to perform to manage different game situations within the group.

Simple Basic Individual Tactics

Serving Tactics (No. 320)
No. 1 rule for beginning players to remember is get the ball over the net. If the ball does not get over the net, it goes over to the other team to try for a point. No. 2 rule is tell your players to make sure they don't step over the line and onto the court as they serve. Young beginning kids should use the "underhand" serve. I have seen too many of them trying the overhand serve, and they usually don't get it over the net. Why

squander a chance to get a point by trying to make a serve they are not good at yet. The side float serve can work for some young players. Explain to your servers that the "contact" point on the hand for all types of serves is the base of the palm.

If they are good at it though have them use the overhand float serve because it is more accurate and fast. The draw back of the "underhand" and "side float" serves are they have to go up in the air over the net then come down, giving the opponent's more time to adjust for the return. Start out by having your beginners aim for the center of the far court with their arm swing until they get better. Then they can aim for a target area.

Passing Tactics (No. 321)
No. 1 rule is try to get in front of the incoming ball by using the correct footwork, and square up to it if at all possible. If it comes in low or mid body, they use a "forearm" pass, or if it's real low they do a "dig" on it. If it's extra low and out of reach, they use the sprawl or roll technique to save it. If the ball comes in high, they use the "overhead" pass technique. Tell them to always know where their setter is located, then pass them the ball rather than to just another player next to them. If coach calls for it, the passer may need to directly "overhead" pass "quick set" to their hitter or spiker in the front row. To get a good "overhead" pass they need to raise their hands to just over the head, palms facing the ball, fingers spread out, thumbs nearly touching, with thumbs and little fingers pointing at 1 or 11 o'clock. Contact is on the finger pads.

Footwork Tactics (No. 322)
No. 1 rule is know which type of footwork to use to move around or get to the ball. Have them use the "hop step" to move forward or backward on shorter distances. Have them use the "slide step" to move laterally

side to side. For mid distances have them use the "open hop step." To move longer distances, like front row to back row, have them use the "crossover step."

Setting Tactics (No. 323)

No. 1 rule is know where your spikers (hitters) are going to be located. First, have them hop step to a balanced position before the ball gets to them. Contact the ball in a slightly crouched position, and on the finger pads in a position above the forehead. Second, as soon as the ball touches the fingers, the ankles, knees, and elbows extend upward and through the ball. Their weight is transferred from the front foot on up to the toes. They rotate their wrists so that their fingers point to the high point of the flight of the ball. This is the front set.

For the "backward set" the technique is similar to the front set. To execute it they turn away from the ball as if to get a pass from behind them. As the ball gets to them and the ankles and knees start to extend upward, they arch their upper back, the elbows move up and back to their ears, and their eyes follow the ball as it is released backward and over their forehead. For the "quick set" the technique is similar to the front set. To execute it they keep their wrists cocked, their elbows move slowly upward, and the ball is directed to a height of only about 1 to 1.5 feet above the net. The idea is the defense has less time to react due to the speed of the attack.

Spiking (Hitting) Tactics (No. 324)

The key to spiking is the timing of the jump. The arm swing is important, but without the right timing of the jump the ball may not go where the spiker wants it, or it may even get blocked. Then you have the fakes which are always cool. The idea is to send the spike to an undefended position on the court, or directly at a weak opponent that will have trouble controlling it. Your players need to use the right mechanics or the ball may go out of bounds or into the net. The general rule for spiking is for your kids to start 15 feet from the net, then gradually work closer to the net as spiking is mastered. Teach your kids the proper arm swing along with the four spiking approach steps. They are:

1. THE TWO STEP APPROACH

Use this method for "quick set" attacks. From standing, leap-hop forward, landing first with the spiking arm foot then the opposite foot. From this base they make their jump.

2. THE THREE STEP APPROACH

Use this for medium speed attacks. Take a normal step with the foot opposite the spiking arm, then in quick succession, leap forward with the spiking hand foot, then the opposite foot. From this base they make their jump.

3. THE FOUR STEP APPROACH

Use this for very high set attacks. Take a small step with the spiking hand foot, then a bigger step with the opposite foot, then leap with the biggest step with the spiking hand foot, and quickly bring it up and plant with the opposite foot. From this base they make their jump.

4. THE SLIDE STEP APPROACH

Use this technique to lose the blocker. It is a four step technique with a pivot. From a middle of the court position the spiker steps at the setter in the front row with the spiking hand foot, then takes a second step toward the setter with the opposite foot. The spiker then pivots and steps parallel to the net with the spiking hand foot. This quick pivoting and side step is what loses the blocker. The opposite foot then takes a final step and leaps upward off one leg as the knee of the spiking hand is lifted. To learn to make a good arm swing see Drills 302-304. Make sure all your attacking spikers know how to do the criss cross faking (see Drill 305).

Tipping Tactics

The key to tipping is the arm swing (see Drill 36). Along with the tipping tactic, teach your hitters how to "tool the block" (see Drill 37), and the roll off technique (see Drill 38).

Offensive Group/Team Tactics

There are a number of offensive set plays and group tactics (Alignments and formations) your team can use to generate scoring There are a number of offensive set plays and group tactics (Alignments and formations) your team can use to generate scoring opportunities. These alignments are designed to put players in a position to confuse your opponent's and score. We won't show every alignment or formation ever invented, but we will show you some of the common alignments and plays to get you going.

This is where all your players put together all the previous skills we mentioned, to work in a play action situation. Most of these are based on a lot of movement and misdirection tactics. You must have a team captain and alternates if the team captain is not playing. The captain is the only player on the team that can speak to the officials, and ask for a clarification on a questionable call. When choosing your captain and alternate, choose a player that is smart, knows the game, and is not a hot "head."

Rotations (No. 325)
Player Positions
Make sure all your players understand their correct position on the court, and how to rotate. Each player must be in the correct position on the court until the ball is contacted on the serve. There are six positions on the court arranged in order at the time of the serve. Players rotate clockwise to the next position. See the diagram for the players in their rotational order.

The three players in the front row are usually considered as potential spikers and blockers. After the serve the players can move anywhere, but at the end of the rally and before the next serve, they must return to their original position if the same server is serving. They must rotate clockwise if the server changes. This will be hard for young beginning players because they forget where they are supposed to be on the court. You will need to do a lot of teaching and showing to get your beginning players learning your system.

Rotations

The rotation of the players proceeds in a clockwise direction. A rotation of more than 6 players may be used. The extra position in the rotation (beyond the 6 on the floor) will be between right forward and the server position. In this case, there can actually be two independent rotations, one for men and one for women. For example, a rotation of 6 men (3 whom play at one time) and 4 women (3 of who play at one time) is allowed. Substitutions following the standard rule may be made for any player in the rotation by a player not in the rotation. In case of injury, if no substitutes not in the rotation are available, a player in the rotation and not currently on the floor may substitute for the injured player (and thus decrease the number of players in the rotation). The injured player may not re-enter the current game. The number of players in a rotation may never drop below 4. It's confusing, but that's the way it is.

Rotation Faults

If an incorrect server serves the ball, your team will lose any points scored by the incorrect server, and your opponent's get to serve. Players that are overlapping are also a fault.

Overlaps

The position of the players before the serve is determined by the position of their feet (See below diagram). As a coach you need to know this. They must be in their correct position until after contact with the serve, at that time they can move to any position anywhere on the court. That does not apply to the server, who can be anywhere behind the end line. A player can not overlap (extend over) the court area of an adjacent player at the time of the serve.

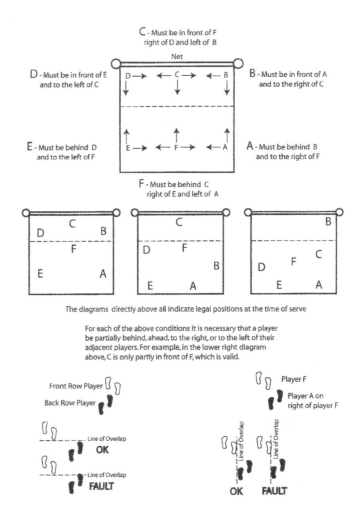

C - Must be in front of F
right of D and left of B

Net

D - Must be in front of E
and to the left of C

B - Must be in front of A
and to the right of C

E - Must be behind D
and to the left of F

A - Must be behind B
and to the right of F

F - Must be behind C
right of E and left of A

The diagrams directly above all indicate legal positions at the time of serve

For each of the above conditions it is necessary that a player
be partially behind, ahead, to the right, or to the left of their
adjacent players. For example, in the lower right diagram
above, C is only partly in front of F, which is valid.

Front Row Player

Back Row Player

Line of Overlap
OK

Line of Overlap
FAULT

Player F

Player A on
right of player F

Line of Overlap

Line of Overlap

OK   FAULT

The rule states that each front row player must have at least part of a
foot closer to the center line dividing the court than both feet of the
corresponding back row player. Also each right or left side player must
have at least part of a foot closer to the right or left sideline than both
feet of the middle player in the corresponding row. Overlaps are illegal
because players must be in their correct rotational order before the
serve. I know this is all sometimes confusing, but that's the way it is.
I'm putting it here because it does effect where you align your players.

Playing the Ball
Each team can contact the ball a maximum of three times in addition to a block. If two or more players contact the ball at the same time, it is considered one contact, and any player may play the ball next. If two opponents contact the ball at the same time and it stays in play, the team receiving the ball can have three more contacts. If the ball goes out of bounds, it is the fault of the team on the opposite side from their contact.

Team Receive Patterns

Passing accuracy is a big part of the success of your offense. So you need to put your team in the most advantageous position areas to accurately receive then pass the ball to the target area for your setter to run the attack. Your team needs to be confident that in each rotation they can prevent your opponent's from scoring points, then get the ball back so that they can serve. Be aware of any potential player overlaps at the moment of the serve. There are basically four serve-receive patterns used in youth volleyball.
They are:

- The 5 player "W" receive pattern.
- The 3 player receive pattern.
- The 4 player receive pattern.
- The 2 player receive pattern.

The "W" Receive Pattern (No. 58)
This is one of the most common receive patterns used in youth volleyball. One of the reasons for this is the players do not need to cover as much ground to pass the ball. This is a good pattern for your young beginning group because they are probably in awe of how big the court is, and they may be a little intimidated at first. This puts 5 players in position to pass the ball to the target player (the setter). The 5 passers line up in the back court in the figure "W."

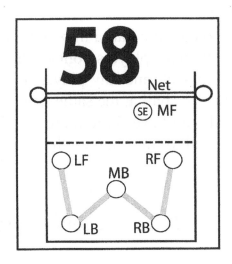

Pattern Advantages

1. There are more passing opportunities for all the players than in other receive patterns.
2. There are not many holes for the opponent's to attack on their serve.
3. This pattern works well for transitioning into either a 4-2, 5-1, or 6-2 offensive alignment.
4. The potential for overlaps is minimal.

Pattern Disadvantages

1. The middle hitters may have trouble getting into their attack positions if they are passing for a quick set in the mid front row.
2. A weak passer can be exploited by a good serving team.

What the Players Do

The two deep players are responsible for passing the deep serves, the three front players are responsible for passing the shorter serves. If the ball is served between the players, the player moving towards the target area has priority and will pass the ball. The setter can be in the front or back row when the ball is served, depending on which alignment they will transition to. They then quickly release to the target area where they will get the pass. This receive pattern can be moved up closer to the net or closer to the end line depending on where the opposing team's serves are going.

Since there are five potential passers in this alignment, communication is vital so that the players don't run into each other, or the ball doesn't drop untouched between players. This will be a challenge for you if you have a young beginning team. Teach them to say things to each other immediately and consistently like, "Mine," "yours," "in" and "out." On deep serves, the front row players should open their lanes (turn sideways to the back row players) to give them a better view of the incoming ball, then get ready to relay the pass.

The 4-Player Receive Pattern (No. 326)
In this pattern there is more court for each of the players to cover and pass the ball than in the 5 player pattern. For this reason the
-1 pattern is not recommended for young teams. There are two alignments for this pattern though. The "U" pattern (-1) and the "diamond" pattern (-2). The -2 pattern has become the most popular pattern now for youth teams. The location designations indicate where the players move from to get into the pattern.

THE "U" PATTERN (-1)
Pattern Advantages
    1. If one player is having trouble passing, this pattern can be used as an adjustment to eliminate that player from the receive pattern.
    2. It moves the middle hitter up, and gives them more time to position themselves for a middle attack.
Pattern Disadvantages
    1. There is a big hole in the middle for opponent's to attack with their serve in the center front of the court.
What the Players Do
The four players in the backcourt are responsible for passing the ball to the setter. The two players in the front court are not involved in the passing.

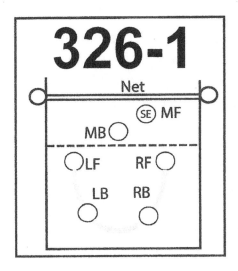

THE "DIAMOND" PATTERN (-2)

Pattern Advantages

1. It's effective because it allows the hitters to move into position for the attack, and it removes the big hole in the middle.

Pattern Disadvantages

1. There is a small hole in the left front for opponent's to attack.

What the Players Do

The four players in the backcourt are responsible for passing the ball to the setter. The two players in the front court don't pass.

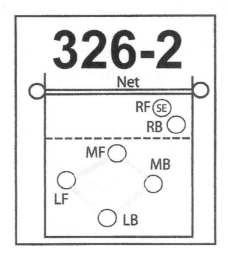

The 3-Player Receive Pattern (No.60)

This pattern was at one time popular in high school and college where you have three good passers. In this pattern there is more court for the passers to cover. For this reason this pattern is not recommended for beginning youth teams. There are two versions of this pattern, the -1 inverted "V," and the -2 shift inverted "V."

THE " INVERTED-V" PATTERN (-1)

Pattern Advantages

    1. There is no hole in the middle for your opponent's to exploit.

    2. You can get your middle hitters into position faster.

    3. You can get your passers out of the receive pattern.

Pattern Disadvantages

    1. The overlap potential is very high. You need to have your players be very aware of their court position before the ball is served.

    2. All three passers have more court to cover than in the 5 or 4 player receive patterns.

What the Players Do

The three players in the middle back court backcourt are responsible for all the passing. One player is out of the receive pattern on the end line, the other is up at the net. The setter stays in the middle target area. The middle back needs to be just a few steps ahead of the left back and the right back.

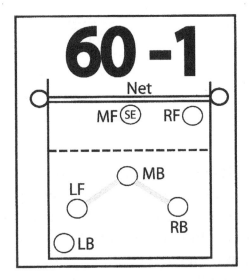

THE "SHIFT STRAIGHT LINE" PATTERN (-2)

Pattern Advantages

1. It's effective because it allows all three of your best passers to handle all the serves.
2. Communication is not the problem it is with the 4 or 5 player receive patterns.
3. It reduces the number of communication problems; fewer players go after the ball.

Pattern Disadvantages

1. There are fewer players to handle the serve.
2. There is a small hole in the left rear corner that your opponent's could attempt to exploit on their serve.

What the Players Do

The three players in the backcourt are responsible for passing the ball to the setter. The three players in the front court are not involved in the passing.

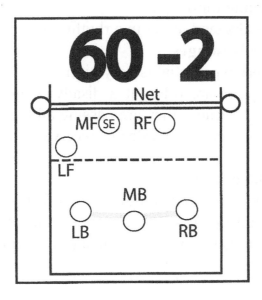

The 2-Player Receive Pattern (No.61)

In this pattern there is more court for each of the players to cover and pass the ball than in the 5, 4, or 3 player patterns. For this reason neither the -1 or -2 pattern is recommended for youth teams. If you have an older advanced team that is very good at passing, you could use these patterns. There are two alignments for this pattern though. The "-1 upside down-L" pattern and the "-2 backward-L" pattern. This pattern frees up hitters in the front row. The location designations indicate where the players move from to get into the pattern.

THE "UPSIDE DOWN-L" PATTERN (-1)

Pattern Advantages

1. Your weaker passers do not need to worry about receiving the serve.
2. With only two passers there is no confusion about who is responsible for the pass.
3. The passers tend to get in a rhythm from passing so often.

Pattern Disadvantages

1. The overlap potential is very high.
2. The passers are often at a disadvantage to get into their hitting positions because they are passing all the time.
3. The short serve is harder to receive with only two players in the pattern.

What the Players Do

The two players in the middle of the backcourt are responsible for passing the ball to the setter. The other four players are not involved in the passing and get in position to make some quick hits.

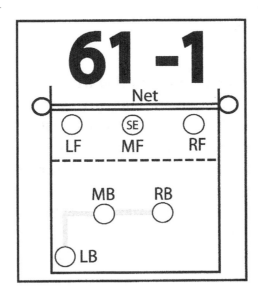

THE "BACKWARD-L" PATTERN (-2)

Pattern Advantages

1. When you can rely on only two players to handle all the serve passes, you free up the rest of the players to focus on their responsibilities.
2. Hitters that don't need to worry about any passing can get in their attacking positions, and be better prepared to make quick hit spikes and kills.

Pattern Disadvantages

1. There is a small hole in the left middle for opponent's to attack.
2. Each passer needs to cover more floor space.

What the Players Do

The two players in the middle of the backcourt are responsible for passing the ball to the setter. The other four players are not involved in the passing.

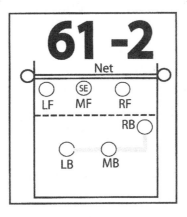

Offensive Systems (Attack Formations)

There are many offensive attack systems to help your team score points, this can kind of overwhelm you and your team when they are just beginning. We won't show you everyone that has ever been invented, but we will show several to choose from. What's going to be hard is choosing the right system to fit your team and their skills. In volleyball they use numbers to label the different offensive systems. The first number refers to how many players are "attackers," and the second number indicates how many players are "setters."

As an example, the 4-2 system has 4 attackers and 2 setters. The 4-2 system is the most popular for young beginning youth teams. In picking an attack system to use, consider the receive pattern you want to use. If your players will need to move all over the court to transition, they will tend to get confused sometimes. Some systems use a front court setter, some use a backcourt setter, and some use a combination of the two.

It's going to be confusing enough for young kids and beginning teams. So I would suggest using one or the other, but not both. I like using one front row center setter personally for young kids, then perfecting your team's skills to execute it. They can set right or left, which tends to confuse young defenses. So pick a system that meshes well with your receive pattern. The three most popular systems are:
- The 4-2 • The 5-1 • The 6-2

The 4-2 System (No.62)
In this system there are four "attackers" and two "setters." We are going to give you three alignments you can shift into for the 4-2. I like the -1 best. You know, the old "K.I.S.S." method.

THE "CENTER SETTER" VARIATION (-1)
System Advantages
1. It is very easy for the two setters to get to their target areas because they don't need to move very far.
2. The overlap potential is very low for beginners.
3. The setter can set right or left.

System Disadvantages
1. The setters will eventually figure out that in this system they will not get to attack and hit, and because of that may not want to play setter.

2. Since the setter is in the front row, there will be only two attackers in the front row at any one time.

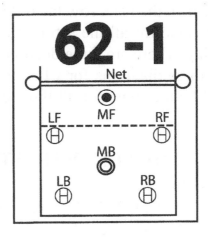

THE "SIDE SETTER" VARIATIONS (-2 & -3)

System Advantages

Same as -1 except, the setter can only set right or left, not both ways.

System Disadvantages

Same as -1.

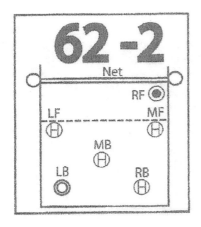
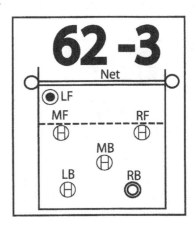

The 5-1 System (No.63)

In this system there are five "attackers" and only one "setter." When the setter is in the front row the 4-2 system is used (see the 62-1 diagram. When the setter is in the back row the 6-2 system is used. Since just one person is responsible for all the setting they need to be very quick and efficient at setting. There are three diagrams for when the setter is in the front row, and three diagrams for when they are in the back row. The advantages will be the same for all three diagrams when the setter is in the front row.

THE "LF" VARIATION (-1)

System Advantages
1. It is very easy for the setter to get to the target area because they don't need to move very far.
2. Making consistent sets is a big advantage for this system. When one setter is responsible for making all the sets, the hitters don't need to adapt as much to where the balls are being set.
3. The setter can easily set to the right or left.

System Disadvantages
1. The setters will eventually figure out that in this system they will not get to attack and hit, and because of that may not want to play setter.
2. Since the setter is in the front row, there will be only two attackers in the front row at any one time.

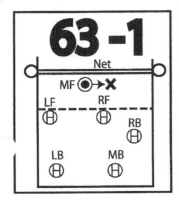 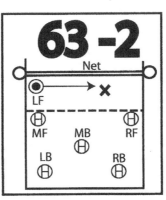 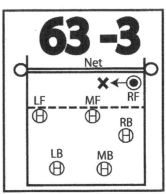

THE "SIDE SETTER" VARIATIONS (-2, -3)

System Advantages

Same as -1 except, the setter can only set right or left, not both ways.

System Disadvantages

Same as -1.

THE "LB" VARIATION (-4)

System Advantages

1. Making consistent sets is a big advantage for this system. When one setter is responsible for making all the sets, the hitters don't need to adapt as much to where the balls are being set.
2. Setters can become attackers when they are at the net, by hitting the ball over the net instead of setting. This is a great surprise attack.

System Disadvantages

1. If the setter is not a good blocker, the defense could be in trouble when the setter is in the front row.
2. When the setter is in the front row, there are only two attackers in the front row unless the setter attacks the pass.

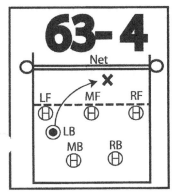 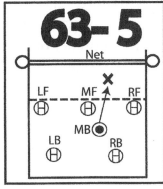 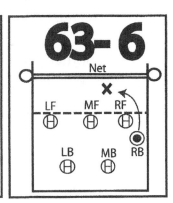

THE "MB & RB SETTER" VARIATIONS (-5, -6)

System Advantages

Same as -4.

System Disadvantages

Same as -4.

The 6-2 System (No.64)

In this system there are six "attackers" and two "setters." The setter comes from the back court to set. It's going to be a little confusing for young beginner teams. There are more rules and things to remember. It's not really a "K.I.S.S." situation for them. However, if your young team is smart you might be able to make it work. When the back court setter rotates to a front row position they become a hitter while the new back court setter sets the next three rotations.

THE "LB" VARIATION (-1)

System Advantages

1. You have three attackers at the net instead of two, and that is a big offensive threat to your opponent's.
2. Your setters become hitters when they rotate to the front row. And kids like that because now the setter gets a chance to hit.

System Disadvantages

1. Because the setter tries to release quickly to get in position, there is a big potential for overlap. This happens when they overlap another player before contact on the serve is made.
2. The setter releases from the back court, and that means they need to cover more distance to get to the target area.

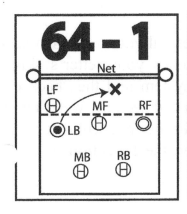 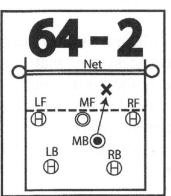 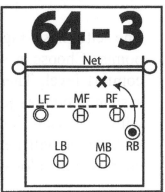

THE "MB & RB SETTER" VARIATIONS (-2 & -3)

System Advantages

Same as -1.

System Disadvantages

Same as -1.

The 6-3 and 6-6 Systems (No.65)

In the 6-3 system there are six hitters and three setters. The three setters set in two rotations, either when they are right back and middle back, or right front and right back. In the 6-6 system there are six hitters and six setters. When the players rotate to a particular position (usually right back) they become the setter for that rotation while in that position. If you have a smart young team you can try these systems. They help develop multiple skills in young players.

System Summations

Make sure you pick a system your kids can handle at their stage of development, and one the meshes smoothly with your serve receive pattern(s). If you have a young team, stick with the simple systems at first like the "W receive pattern then transitioning into a 5-1 system.

Read the advantages and disadvantages of each system to see how they might mesh with your team.

The setter has a big influence on how successful your team is at scoring points. Choose a setting system that matches your setter's skill and comfort level. There is the "front court" system and the "back court" system. You may just need to try them both and see how well they work with your team. Sometimes after working in the front court for a while your setter will get comfortable there, then the transition to the back court will go a lot smoother.

The Front Court Setter.

This alignment places the setter in the front court. Keep the following points in mind when you use this alignment:
- Incorporate strong attacking skills.
- Use Surprise Attacks.
- Reduce any pressure on your setter.
- Minimize Movement.

Incorporate strong attacking skills

Once the opponent's see which system you are using every time they might employ a double block on your hitter every time. They only have two hitters to defend against. So you need to teach your hitters up front to be strong and very confident. Teach them a variety of shots to use, it will make them more successful. Tips, off speed attacks, that type of skill .

Use surprise attacks

This is a great way to counter having fewer hitter in the front row. Every once in a while have your setter take the pass and spike the ball. It will really surprise the opposition, and make them rethink the double block all the time. You could even have you two front row hitters do some fakes going in the opposite way. And even occasionally have your setter look like they might spike one way, then "back set" the other way to one of the front hitters.

Reduce any pressure on your setter

Generally your setter has only two attacking options in the front row, which eliminates a lot of decision making for young beginning setters who are learning the position. Also they can pass the ball to a back row setter in some situations. All of this reduces pressure on the front row setter.

Minimize movement

In the front court alignment the setter usually only needs to take a few steps to get in position to receive the ball. Minimizing the movement they need to make eliminates a lot of bad hits because they are more likely to be ready when the ball gets to them.

The Back Court Setter.

This alignment places the setter in the back court, but they are still close to the front court because they move up a little. Keep the following points in mind when you use this alignment:

• Recognize the defensive positioning.
• Be creative.

Recognize the defensive positioning

Having three hitters up in the front row will make it more difficult for the opponents to double your hitters. Teach your setter to recognize which hitters the opponents tend to double team, then they can adjust and set to one of the other hitters.

Be creative

With three hitters in the front row you have many attacking options to choose from. Teach them to distribute the ball around to all the hitters during a match instead of setting the same player or location over and over. Have one of your assistants track where the setter makes their set every time during a match. Then use the statistics to help your setter become more efficient by showing them what they did. You may find that your setter is making more sets to a specific area or player, then talk to them and have them make some adjustments. This way they won't become predictable. Explain the importance of deception. Fakes are good in any alignment, but they can be very effective in this alignment.

If you have each of your front row hitter step towards the net on every set and launch themselves in the air, regardless of whether the ball is being set their way, your opponent's will need to defend each one of them. This takes away their double blocks. This means your hitters will only need to deal with a single block on the majority of their hits. Here is another concept to consider, the "full court attack." This is when everyone on the court attacks. You need to remind them though that when a back row player attacks that they can not jump in front of the attack line. Can you imagine being on the other side of the net and seeing all the players jumping up on a set and coming at you. This has to just overwhelm a young team.

Play Movement

No Blockers
3 On 3- Front Court Sets (No.66)
This is three on three at the net, opponent's are not using blockers. This can be used with any system with setter on the right side, left side, or in the middle, and two hitters in the front row. When the setter is on the LF, everything is flip-flopped or opposite. Even when the other hitter gets the set, the other player fakes going to the net. When the setter is in the middle, it opens things up for lots of fakes. In 66-6 system the LF hitter goes behind the setter, and fakes a hit in the right corner. The RF hitter lets the LF hitter clear, then goes behind the setter and makes the spike in the right corner. Then at any time the setter can just turn and spike or tip right over the net off the pass.

144

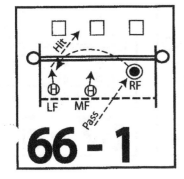 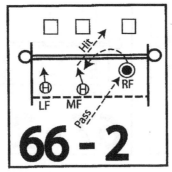 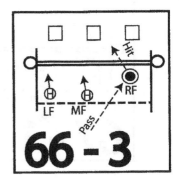

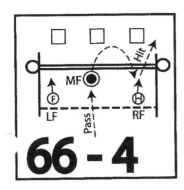 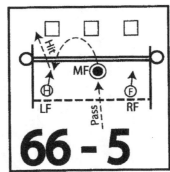 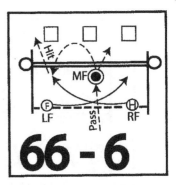

3 On 3- Back Court Sets (No.67)

This is three on three at the net, opponent's are not using blockers. This can be used with any system with setter making a set from any one of the back court positions. This changes everything and gives you more options with three hitters in the front row instead of two. Your setter can set from any of back court positions.

And they can set to the LF, MF, or RF. Or you can have single fake hits or multiple fake hits. No matter who the set goes to, the other two hitters in the front row run up to the net and jump up (the fake hit). In 67-4 to 67-6 the fake hitter goes first and the real hitter goes second right behind them. Work on the timing for the fakes in practice.

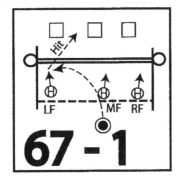 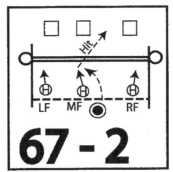 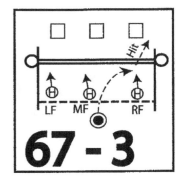

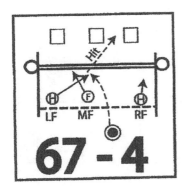 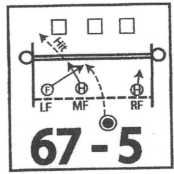 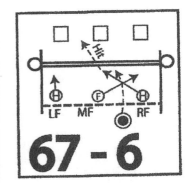

6 On 6- Full Court Attacks (No.68)

This is a six on six full court attack where any of the back court players can make the hit. This can be used with any system with the setter making a set from anywhere on the court. Remind your players that when they make the hit from the back court that they can not jump in front of the attack line. As you can see there are a lot of possible options. I have just shown a few so that you get the idea. The setter can be in the front court or the back court. A player in the front court makes a fake jump one way, and the hitter makes the hit in another direction (misdirection faking).

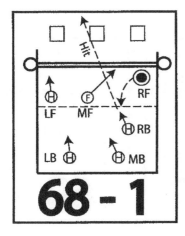 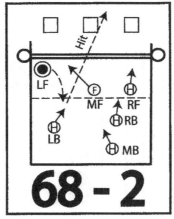 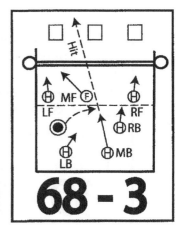

Against Blockers
3 On 3- Front Court Sets (No.69)

The first thing to determine is your opponent always using a single blocker, or are the using a double block defense. You can't reset your offensive attack unless you determine this. First we will give you some ideas against a double team block, then against a single blocker. This depends more on where the hitter is rather than where the setter is. What you need to teach your players is look for and attack the holes. When your opponent's are using a double block, especially way over to one side, there has to be a hole somewhere. Teach your hitters to find it. If the opponent's are successful with a double block, have your hitters just roll the ball off to the side of the blockers hands.

If your opponent's are continually double team blocking your hitters up in the front row, go to some back row hitting over their head (see No.68 plays). If your opponent's are continually single blocking your hitters up in the front row, go to the back row sets (see No. 67 plays). Have your front row hitters do a lot of criss cross fakes and hits. It's going to be 3 on 3, so have your hitters look for holes between their front row players. Three hitters in the front row will make it harder for your opponent's to double team block.

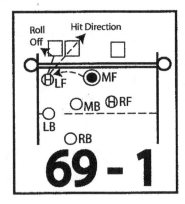 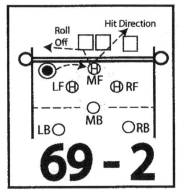 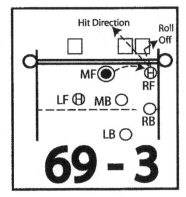

15. Offensive Training/Learning Games

These are learning games you can have your team play once in a while. This will break up your practice from what seem to young players like endless hours of monotonous drills. While playing these games your kids are learning a core training skill, and having a little fun.

Hit the Square Serving Game (No. 82)
Object of the game :
Hit the ball into one of the four quadrants using an overhand or underhand serve.
Goal: To improve on their serving accuracy.
The game basics are : This is a 2 vs 2 game. You will need a volleyball court, either indoors or outdoors. You will need 2 players per side. Divide the court up into four quadrants per side using tape on the floor or cones. It takes more time to set up, but tape is better. If you use tape have some of your coaches or kids help you mark the court. Have an assistant coach get a pad of paper and keep score for each server. Award points for the regular scoring rules. Give additional or extra

points for; Give 5 points for calling the quadrant your serve will go into. Give 2 points for serving into either of the back quadrants. Give 1 point for serving into either of the front quadrants. Give points even if the ball is returned. First player to get 25 points wins the game, no ties.

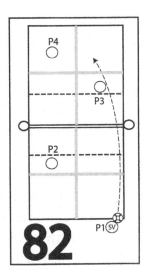

Playing the game :
Players try to return the serve and volley just like in a regular game. Each server gets 3 serve attempts to make points, then rotate servers. When the game is over move on to another drill. The next time you play the game give 4 different players a chance to play. The kids not playing can be working on a drill with another coach, instead of just standing around.

To make the game easier :
Give points for any serve that makes it over the net, even if it goes out of bounds. Lower the net for the little beginning kids.

To make the game harder :
Only give points if the server can call, then hit, their quadrant. Only give points if the serve hits the floor in the quadrant called. Reduce the size of the court or increase the number of target areas to 6 or 9 per side.

King of the Court Serving Game (No. 83)

Object of the game :

See how many times players can hit the ball over the net without missing.

Goal:

To improve on their serving accuracy, and get the ball over the net every time.

The game basics are :

This is a competitive game. You will need a volleyball court, either indoors or outdoors. To save time you will need 2 players per side. Just for fun have two assistant coaches or parents get a pad of paper and keep track of how many consecutive times each player gets the ball over the net, without hitting it, and within the bounding lines. This is a process of elimination. They can use any type of serve they like. When a player hits or tips the net with a serve, or it goes out of bounds they are out of the game. The last player left without any misses over the net wins the game (King of the Court).

Playing the game :

Players stand back at the end line and try to serve the ball over the net. It can land anywhere in the opposite court (short - long whatever) as long as it does not hit the net, and stays within bounds. Players take turns serving, by alternating one after the other around clockwise, not all at once, and to their left. When a player does go out they move back and let another player try. When there is a winner, have all players move on to another drill. While players wait you could have them working on a drill nearby with another coach, then rotate players from one activity to the other so that nobody is standing around.

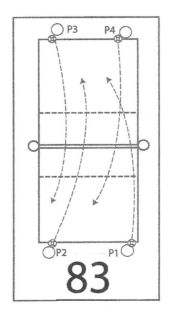

To make the game easier :
Have beginning players move up 5 feet closer to the net. Mark it with cones. Lower the net.

To make the game harder :
Have players move back 5 feet farther away from the end line. They need to make a certain type of serve, like overhead style, or even side arm, but not underhand.

Wall Passing Shuttle Game (No.86)
Object of the game :
To make a pass into a square marked way up on a wall, then go to the end of the line while the next player steps up and passes it up in the square without the ball hitting the ground. Team tries to see how long they can keep it going from player to player.

Goal:
To improve on their passing accuracy and quickness to get to the ball.

The game basics are :

This is a fun game that involves teamwork. You will need a volleyball and a wall, either indoors or outdoors. Mark a 12 inch or 18 inch square up on a wall with tape. Depending on the size of your kids, the bottom should be about 3 - 4 feet over the top of their head.

Playing the game :

The first player in line stands about 4 feet away from the wall and starts it out by passing the ball up into the square, then gets quickly out of the way and goes to the end of the line. Mark a line 4 feet away from the wall with tape. The next player in line quickly moves up, catches the pass, then immediately passes it back up into the square without it falling to the floor. This keeps going on from player to player until it falls to the floor. It will take teamwork to keep it going up. You can even have the player making the pass call out it's number so that their teammates can tell the consecutive number of passes that have been made. The passes can be forearm or overhead.

To make the game easier :

Move a little closer to the wall for the little kids, and lower the square a little.

To make the game harder :

Move a little farther away from the wall. Players can only use a forearm pass.

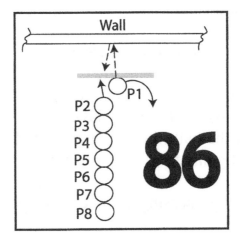

Pass in the Can Game (No.87)

Object of the game :

To make a forearm pass into one of three garbage or trash cans placed at the net, to score points for their team.

Goal:

To improve on their forearm passing accuracy.

The game basics are :

This is a fun game that involves a little teamwork. You will need a volleyball court, a volleyball, and three big large garbage or trash cans. There are four players to a team, one server and three passers. The teamwork comes in by the server making a good high serve to one of their teammates standing in the back court. A low over the net type serve is not going to work. The teammate then tries to forearm pass the ball into one of the garbage cans. If players do not arc their pass, the ball may not fall into the can. Give the team 2 points every time a ball goes into the can (even if it bounces out). Each team gets served 5 balls, then add up the team points for that round. Have a coach keep track of the points for each team on a pad of paper.

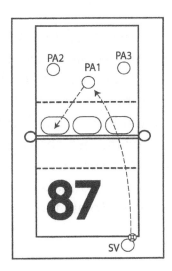

To make the game easier :

Have the server come up in mid court and toss the ball over the net

To make the game harder :
Have only one can to aim for, then move it way over to one side where it will be harder to aim for. Or use smaller can(s).

Crazy Passes Game (No.88)
Object of the game :
For a setter to make passes from a serve back and forth to two of the three passers in the backcourt, then the setter can overhead pass or hit the ball over the net. The setter passes in order first to PA1 passer, then to the third PA3 passer. If they can do this they are awarded points.
Goal:
To improve on their forearm passing accuracy.
The game basics are :
The is played 4 vs 4. This is a fun game that involves a little teamwork and accuracy. You will need a volleyball court, a volleyball, and four players on each side. There are three passers, and one server/setter on a team. All passes must be forearm passes. When each of the three players can complete a forearm pass back to the setter, the team gets 2 points. Have a coach with a pad of paper keep track of the points for each team.
Playing the game :
The server can use an overhand or underhand serve. If the receiving team fails to get the three forearm passes to their setter, the rally stops and the receiving team becomes the serving team. When the receiving team does make their three passes and the ball goes back over the net, the other team rallies and tries to get the ball back over the net. If they do get the ball back over the net, the original team rallies When a rally is finally finished, alternate serves regardless of who wins the rally, and the other team gets a chance to make points. Make sure each team gets an equal number of serves. Rotate the players on each team after a rally.

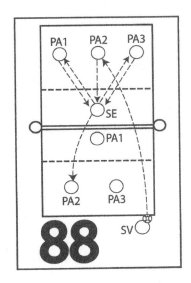

To make the game easier :
Let each team have five serve chances to make their three successful passes to their setter.
To make the game harder :
Play 3 vs 3.

It's Hammer Time Game (No.89)
Object of the game :
Try to spike the ball over the net without it going out of bounds.
This gets the team points.
Goal:
To improve on their spiking accuracy and technique.
The game basics are :
The is played 3 vs 3. This is a fun game that almost all kids like. You will need a volleyball court, a volleyball, and three players on each side. There is one passer, one setter, and one hitter on a team. Teams must use a three touch attack. Give 1 point if the ball is spiked and hits the net or goes out of bounds. Give 2 points if the ball is spiked and stays in

play. Give 3 points if the ball is spiked and it ends the rally. Have a coach with a pad of paper keep track of the points for each team.

Playing the game :

Team "A" serves to team "B." Then play is continuous until the rally ends by the ball touching the floor. The server can use an overhand or underhand serve. Alternate the serve between the teams, no matter who wins the rally. Make sure each team gets an equal number of serves. And rotate players on each team after each rally ends.

Game Variations :

Play the game using other types of hits, such as "down the line," "cross court," or "tips."

To make the game easier :

Play 5 vs 5, or 6 vs 6. Lower the net for the little beginning kids.

To make the game harder :

Only give points for spikes that end a rally.

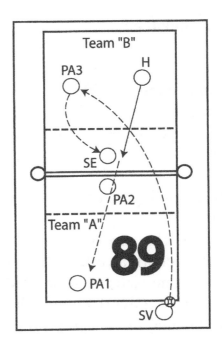

Hit the Square Game (No.90)
Object of the game :

Each side of the court is divided up into six zones. Players try to hit the ball into one of the zones, using a spike, an off speed spike, a tip, or a down ball. By hitting some zones they can score more points than in others.

Goal:

To improve on their hitting accuracy and technique and the ability to place the hit where they want it to go.

The game basics are :

The game is played 3 vs 3. This is a fun game that almost all kids like. You will need a volleyball court, a volleyball, and three players on each side. There is one passer, one setter, and one hitter on a team. Give 2 points for hitting the back corner zones. Give 1 point for hitting the front three zones or the back center zone. Have a coach with a pad of paper keep track of the points for each team.

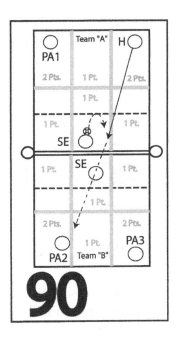

Playing the game :

Team "A" starts with their setter making a set for their hitter, who tries to hit the ball into the zone with the most points. Let each team use overhead or forearm passes to get the ball over the net. Then play is continuous until the rally ends by the ball touching the floor. Only give points when the ball is hit over the net to the other side. After the rally ends, switch sides and the other team sets. Make sure each team gets an equal number of sets. Rotate players on both sides after a rally ends. Play the game for 30 minutes, then move on to another drill.

To make the game easier :

Lower the net for the little beginning kids.

To make the game harder :

Have players call which zone their hit is going into, then give them extra points if they make it. Only give points if the ball hits the floor of a target zone. Use a nine zone target variation system as shown.

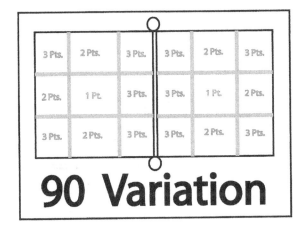

Hitter War Game (No.91)
Object of the game :

Each side has a designated back court hitter. They are the only one that can score points by getting a clean kill.

158

Goal:

To improve on their back court hitting accuracy technique, and the on their back court hitting accuracy and technique, and the ability to place the hit where they want it to go, getting it cleanly over the net.

The game basics are :

The game is played 6 vs 6. This is a fun game that almost all kids like. You will need a volleyball court, a volleyball, and six players on each side. Only one back court hitter is designated on each team. Outside back vs outside back, or middle back vs middle back. Only that player on each side can score points with a clean kill. Have a coach with a pad of paper keep track of the points. Play until five points are scored then move on to another drill.

Playing the game :

Coach tosses a ball in to one team, they start a rally just like a regular game. Then try to get the ball to the designated hitter in the back court who can score a point. The game is played like a regular game with the same rules, except for who can score the point. If a player other than the designated player ends the rally no point is given, but that side gets the ball. Rotate the players on each team after the rally ends. Play the game for 40 minutes then move on.

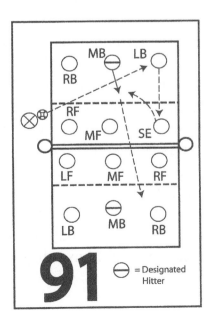

159

To make the game easier :
Lower the net for the little beginning kids.
To make the game harder :
Have players call which zone their hit is going into, then they have to make it.

Down and Up Digging Game (No.92)
Object of the game :
Start one meter in from the end line, receive a long pass just in front of them, then dig the ball over a rope suspended over the attack line. And also try to dig it over the net for a point.
Goal:
To improve on their digging accuracy and technique, and the ability to get to the ball, place the dig where they want it to go, getting it cleanly over the net.
The game basics are :
The game is played 2 vs 2. Receiving team players line up 1 meter in from the end line at a starting line. A rope is held up 6 feet to 8 feet in the air, over the top of the attack line by coaches, parents, or players, and parallel to the net on both sides of the court. Have a coach get a pad of paper and keep track of the score.
Playing the game :
Player P2 on one team starts the game by toss serving the ball over the net so that it lands just in front of the starting line, and the player receiving it has to move forward to dig it. Their dig must get over the rope on their side, and into the opponent's side. If they get the ball over the rope to the opponent's side they get 1 point. If the toss goes past the starting line it is considered out of bounds, and the ball goes over to the opponent's to toss. The player receiving the ball must stay behind the starting line until after the ball has been tossed so that they are forced to dig the ball. When working with the younger kids, coach may need to stand on a platform and toss the ball to the player that will dig the ball because younger kids may not have the skills to place the ball where it needs to go.

160

Once the dig gets over the net both teams start to rally just like a regular game and same rules. The rally play does not need to go over the rope though. So the players holding the rope can move it up next to the net where it will be out of the way until the rally ends, then move it back. Alternate the toss side when the rally is over, regardless of who wins the rally. Rotate the players on each team after the rally ends. Make sure each team gets an equal number of serve tosses. Play the game to five points, then move on.

To make the game easier or more continuous :

Lower the net and rope for the younger beginning kids. Increase the number of players.

To make the game harder :

Continue regular play after the dig point has been made, then go to regular point type scoring. Move the starting line for the dig farther back.

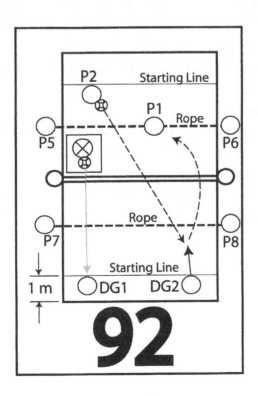

The Quick Set Game (No.94)
Object of the game :
To make quick sets 2 feet above the net off of coaches tosses, first to one side then the other, and get points.
Goal:
To improve on their quick setting accuracy and technique, going to either side from MF position.
The game basics are :
This is a little quick setting game to earn points. Coach starts out by tossing balls up in the air to a setter at the middle front position. The setter needs to make a quick set, first to their right then their left. The quick set needs to be up just 2 feet above the top of the net. Give 2 points for a two foot set, give 1 point for any other set that is higher.
Playing the game :
On coaches toss the setter tries to get their set just 2 feet above the net. The first toss they set to their right, the next toss to their left. Each player gets 4 sets. Have a coach get a pad of paper and keep track of the points for each player. Let each player get two 4 set chances, then move on to another drill.
Game Variations :
You can also play the game where the setter needs to make a "high outside set" or a "back set" for points.
To make the game easier :
Coach can get closer to toss for the younger kids, where it will be easier for them to get under the toss. Or lower the net a little.

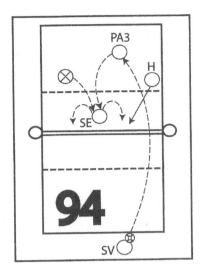

To make the game harder :

Coach can move farther away, and toss the ball, where it will harder for the setter to get under the ball. Have a server hit the ball over the net to a passer, who passes the ball to the setter. You can even have a hitter come in, jump up, and fake swing a hit.

King of the Court Setting Game (No.95)
Object of the game :

To make as many style points as possible, and be king of the setters.

Goal:

To improve on their setting accuracy, technique, and consistency.

The game basics are :

This is a little rapid fire setting game to earn style points (See No.94 game diagram). Coach starts out by tossing balls up in the air to a setter at the middle front position. The setter needs to make a rapid set to either side. Give 2 points for a near perfect set, give 1 point for any other set that is decent. They need to get under the ball to make their set. If they miss the toss they get no points.

Playing the game :

On coaches toss the setter tries to make a high outside set. If the set goes high up and comes down near the outside hitting position, they get their 2 points, if not they only get 1 point. Coach tells the player where they want them to stand for the set. Each player gets 5 consecutive attempts each round. Let each player get two sets of 5 attempts, then move on another drill.

Game Variations :

You can also play the game where the setter needs to make a "quick set" or a "back set" for points.

To make the game easier :

Coach can get closer to toss for the younger kids, where it will be easier for them to get under the toss.

To make the game harder :

Coach can move farther away, and toss the ball, where it will harder for the setter to get under the ball. Have a server hit the ball over the net to a passer, who passes the ball to the setter. You can even have a hitter come in, jump up, and fake swing a hit.

The Footwork Game (No.97)

Object of the game :

To make leap hops all the way across court, then come back to their starting point making slide steps, to earn style points.

Goal:

To improve on their footwork technique, speed, and consistency.

The game basics are :

This is a little rapid fire footwork game to earn points for style. Players start out on coaches whistle then leap hop all the way across the court as fast and accurate as they can, then they make a quick stop and slide step back the other way to the starting point as fast as they can. Make sure players know this game is more for their footwork technique than their speed. The speed will come, but first they need to get their footwork down. Give 1 point for a decent attempt. Give 2 points for a near perfect attempt. They get no points if they fall down or use hardly any or sloppy footwork. Have a coach with a pad of paper keep track of the score, and determine style technique accuracy.

Playing the game :

Coach needs to demonstrate the correct footwork to use on both steps before starting the game. On coaches whistle the first player starts across, hands up, facing the net. They go across using one type of step, come back still facing the net using the other step. Down and back is one set, then they go to the end of the line. Make sure that each player gets to do at least two sets, then after 30-40 minutes move on another drill.

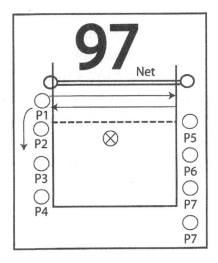

Game Variations :

You can also play the game by switching out with a "crossover step" or adding it to a set.

To make the game easier :

Coach can stop and re-demonstrate to the younger kids if they are NOT doing the steps correctly.

To make the game harder :

Have them switch to another step half way across, and half way back.

Up in the Air Digging Game (No.98)
Object of the game :
To see how long players can keep the ball up in the air without dropping it.
Goal:
To improve on their digging abilities.
The game basics are :
Place your kids in two player teams. This is two partners in a digging position passing the ball back and forth, while on their knees. They attempt to keep the ball up in the air as long as they can by digging the ball
Playing the game :
Two partners get on their knees and face each other, at about 10 feet apart. They put their hands and forearms together in the digging position, then when coach blows their whistle they start passing it back and forth. Coach times them to see which team can keep it up in the air the longest. The team keeping it up in the air the longest, wins the game. You can do more than one team at a time if you have someone to time and watch them. Get a parent to help if necessary.

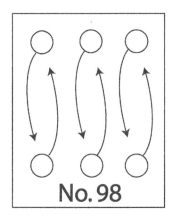

No. 98

To make the game easier :
Bring the players in closer together.

To make the game harder :
Move the players farther apart.
Time of the game :
Play for only about 30 minutes, depending on how many kids you have.

16.Sample Practice Schedules

Practice Rituals

Closing Ritual (No.106)
Object of the information: To help your kids feel a sense of closure after practices and games.
Why Have a Closing Ritual: The "Positive Coaching Alliance (PCA)," of which I am a member, recommends this as an end to practices. This is a brief gathering where coaches and players signify the end of the days activity, and provide a transition back to life without sports. This is a time to remind them of the next practice, or a coming Game time and date. Make sure you let them know they did a good job during the day's practice. And last everyone puts their hands up in the air together in the center of the group and on the command, "Ready," they all together yell " Yeah Team," or something like that. Your kids will know what to say.

Practices

Practice Schedules (No.107)
Object of the information: To stress the importance of setting up a practice schedule to get more training in during practices.
Why Have Practice Schedules: When you lay out a practice schedule, kids learn more, and faster (Practice is usually 2 hours for beginners). You can't always follow it to the letter, but try to follow it as close as possible within reason. I know many of you coaches don't like to follow a schedule, but if you do, you are going to find that the young kids learn a lot more. It makes the learning process quicker, and their skills improve much faster. The secret is plan out what you want to teach each

session, then get some assistant coaches to help. First thing to do is get yourself a dedicated to volleyball calendar. Mark all your practice dates and times down for a master schedule, then make copies and give them to your players. I want to point out something here these practice schedules are not etched in stone, The practice schedules I am showing are just for giving you some ideas on how to plan them. Also make sure you have practice cancellation telephone number to call in case it is necessary.

Coaches

Get as many as possible. They can even be parents, who may just be sitting around doing nothing all the way through practice while just watching anyway. Might as well put them to work. It's not hard if you just show them exactly what it is you want them to do. I do this all the time. And I find that many parents are willing to help as long as you show them EXACTLY what it is you want them to do. We will put some different types of one hour sample schedules together for you to see some different ways how to do it. The idea is to show you how to teach larger groups the same fundamentals in 2 days instead of maybe 3 or 4. If you can only get on the practice court 1 or 2 days a week, then see if you can find a gym with a net open someplace to get extra practices. Young kids need lots of practice to really learn the fundamental better. There is a lot more to learn when you don't have much practice time.

Practice Area

A lot of these drills can be run out in a grass area. Some Leagues will only let you practice 2 times a week when school is in session. During the summer, many youth teams practice every day if possible and they can find the space. Typically teams will work with the nearest School program to share their court. I think it's best to work on a full size court with a net if you can find one. When you work with the local School, they will also usually let you share their equipment, as long as you take care of it. They will also have lights so that you can work after dark. It gives you lots more options.

Practice Schedules

We will take the middle of the road and show some sample 1 hour schedules for you to look at. They are based on evening practices with the younger kids. The time can always be adjusted for day practices or other times. They are also based on half your squad practicing offensive fundamentals, while the other half works on defense.

1 Hour Sample Schedules
METHOD 1- BEGINNERS
(Group of up to 15)

Practice 1 (One Coach, Two Assistants)
The *Focus is on Footwork*

Coach Plus Assistants (Whole Group)
4:30 to 4:35. Jumping jacks to loosen up
4:35 to 4:40 Warm Up and Stretching
4:40 to 4:55 Leap hopping training
4:55 to 5:00 **Water Break** Whistle blows to start and end
5:00 to 5:15 Slide stepping training
5:15 to 5:30 Crossover stepping training
5:30 to 5:35 Short Talk and Closing Ritual

Practice 2 (One Coach, Two Assistants)
The *Focus is on Passing*

Coach Plus Assistants (Whole Group)
4:30 to 4:35. Jumping jacks to loosen up
4:35 to 4:40 Warm Up and Stretching
4:40 to 4:55 Basic forearm passing training
4:55 to 5:00 **Water Break** Whistle blows to start and end
5:00 to 5:15 Basic overhead passing training
5:15 to 5:30 Passing to the setter training
5:30 to 5:35 Short Talk and Closing Ritual

METHOD 2- BEGINNERS
(Group of up to 20)

Practice 1 (One Coach, Three Assistants)
The *Focus is on Footwork and Passing*

NOTE: Split into Two Groups (Stations)

Group 1, 2 Altogether
4:30 to 4:35. Jumping jacks to loosen up
4:35 to 4:40 Warm Up and Stretching
                Whistle blows to go to First Station

Coach Plus Assistant Station1 (Up to 10 Kids)
4:40 to 4:55 Leap hopping training with Gp.1
4:55 to 5:00 **Water Break** Whistle blows to start and end
                Whistle blows to Rotate Group to next Station (No.2)
5:00 to 5:15 Slide stepping training with Gp.2
5:15 to 5:30 Crossover stepping training with Gp.2
                WhistlebBlows to gather for End of Practice
5:30 to 5:35 Short talk and closing ritual (All together)

Asst.No.1 Plus Assistant Station 2 (Up to10 Kids)
4:40 to 4:55 Basic forearm passing training with Gp.2
4:55 to 5:00 **Water Break** Whistle blows to start and end
                Whistle blows to Rotate Group to next Station (No.1)
5:00 to 5:15 Basic overhead passing training with Gp.1
5:15 to 5:30 Passing to setter training with Gp.1
                Whistle blows to gather for End of Practice
5:30 to 5:35 Short talk and closing ritual (All together)

Practice 2 (One Coach, Three Assistants)
The *Focus is on Spiking and Tipping*

NOTE: Split into Two Groups (Stations)

Group 1, 2 Altogether
4:30 to 4:35. Jumping jacks to loosen up
4:35 to 4:40 Warm Up and Stretching
                Whistle blows to go to First Station

Coach Plus Assistant Station1 (Up to10 Kids)
4:40 to 4:55 Three part lead up footwork training with Gp.1
4:55 to 5:00 **Water Break** Whistle blows to start and end
                Whistle blows to rotate group to next Station (No.2)
5:00 to 5:15 Three part footwork training with Gp.2
5:15 to 5:30 Kneeling spike training with Gp.2
                Whistle blows to gather for End of Practice
5:30 to 5:35 Short talk and closing ritual (All together)

Asst.No.1 Plus Assistant Station 2 (Up to 10 Kids)
4:40 to 4:55 Tip in training, with Gp.2
4:55 to 5:00 **Water Break** Whistle blows to start and end
           Whistle blows to rotate group to next Station (No.2)
5:00 to 5:15 Roll off the block training with Gp.1
5:15 to 5:30 Tooling a block training with Gp.1
           Whistle blows to gather for End of Practice
5:30 to 5:35 Short talk and closing ritual (All together)

METHOD 3- BEGINNERS
(Groups of up to 21)

Practice 1 (One Coach, Five Assistants)
The *Focus is on Spiking, Tipping, Digging*

NOTE: Split into Three Groups (Stations)

Group 1, 2 ,3 Altogether
4:30 to 4:35. Jumping jacks to loosen up
4:35 to 4:40 Warm Up and Stretching
           Whistle blows to go to First Station

Coach Plus Assistant Station1 (Up to 7 Kids)
4:40 to 4:55 Three part footwork training with Gp.1
4:55 to 5:00 **Water Break** Whistle blows to start and end
           Whistle blows to rotate group to next Station (No.2)
5:00 to 5:15 Three part footwork training with Gp.3
           Whistle blows to rotate group to next Station (No.2)
5:15 to 5:30 Three part footwork training with Gp.2
           Whistle blows to gather for End of Practice
5:30 to 5:35 Short talk and closing ritual (All together)

Asst.No.1 Plus Assistant Station 2 (Up to 7 Kids)
4:40 to 4:55 Tipping training with Gp.2
4:55 to 5:00 **Water Break** Whistle blows to start and end
           Whistle blows to rotate group to next Station (No.3)
5:00 to 5:15 Tipping training with Gp.3
           Whistle blows to rotate group to next Station (No.3)
5:15 to 5:30 Tipping training with Gp.1
           Whistle blows to gather for End of Practice
5:30 to 5:35 Short talk and closing ritual (All together)

Asst.No.2 Plus Assistant Station 3 (Up to 7 Kids)
4:40 to 4:55 Basic Digging training with Gp.3
4:55 to 5:00 **Water Break** Whistle blows to start and end
           Whistle blows to rotate group to next Station (No.1)
5:00 to 5:15 Partner digging drill training with Gp.2
           Whistle blows to rotate group to next Station (No.1)
5:15 to 5:30 Dig and cover drill training with Gp.1
           Whistle blows to gather for End of Practice
5:30 to 5:35 Short talk and closing ritual (All together)

Practice 6 (One Coach, Five Assistants)
The ***Focus is on Serving and Team Play***

NOTE: Split into Three Groups (Stations)

Group 1, 2 ,3 Altogether
4:30 to 4:35. Jumping jacks to loosen up
4:35 to 4:40 Warm Up and Stretching
                             Whistle blows to go to First Station

Coach Plus Assistant Station1 (Up to 7 Kids)
4:40 to 4:55 Underhand Serve training with Gp.1
4:55 to 5:00 **Water Break** Whistle blows to start and end
                             Whistle blows to rotate group to next Station (No.2)
5:00 to 5:15 Side float serve training with Gp.3
                             Whistle blows to rotate group to next Station (No.2)
5:15 to 5:30 Overhand float serve training with Gp.2
                             Whistle blows to gather for End of Practice
5:30 to 5:35 Short talk and closing ritual (All together)

Asst.No.1 Plus Assistant Station 2 (Up to 7 Kids)
4:40 to 4:55 Side float Serve training with Gp.2
4:55 to 5:00 **Water Break** Whistle blows to start and end
                             Whistle blows to rotate group to next Station (No.3)
5:00 to 5:15 Jump serve training with Gp.1
                             Whistle blows to rotate group to next Station (No.3)
5:15 to 5:30 Roundhouse serve training with Gp.3
                             Whistle blows to gather for End of Practice
5:30 to 5:35 Short talk and closing ritual (All together)

Asst.No.2 Plus Assistant Station 3 (Up to 7 Kids)
4:40 to 4:55 Team plays training with Gp.3
4:55 to 5:00 **Water Break** Whistle blows to start and end
                             Whistle blows to rotate group to next Station (No.1)
5:00 to 5:15 Team plays training with Gp.2
                             Whistle blows to rotate group to next Station (No.1)
5:15 to 5:30 Team plays training with Gp.1
                             Whistle blows to gather for End of Practice
5:30 to 5:35 Short talk and closing ritual (All together)

METHOD 4- BEGINNERS
(Whole Team)

Later On Practice (One Coach, Five Assistants)
The *Focus is on Team Plays and Games*

NOTE: Split into Three Groups (Stations)

Group 1, 2 ,3 Altogether
4:30 to 4:35. Jumping jacks to loosen up
4:35 to 4:40 Warm Up and Stretching
　　　　　　　Whistle blows to go to First Station

Coach Plus Assistant Station1 (Up to 7 Kids)
4:40 to 4:55 Specific team plays No.1 with Gp.1
4:55 to 5:00 **Water Break** Whistle blows to start and end
　　　　　　　Whistle blows to rotate group to next Station (No.2)
5:00 to 5:15 Specific team plays No.2 with Gp.3
　　　　　　　Whistle blows to rotate group to next Station (No.2)
5:15 to 5:30 Specific team plays No.3 with Gp.2
　　　　　　　Whistle blows to gather for end of practice
5:30 to 5:35 Short talk and closing ritual (All together)

Asst.No.1 Plus Assistant Station 2 (Up to 7 Kids)
4:40 to 4:55 Specific plays No.2 with Gp.2
4:55 to 5:00 **Water Break** Whistle blows to start and end
　　　　　　　Whistle blows to rotate group to next Station (No.3)
5:00 to 5:15 Specific plays No.3 with Gp.1
　　　　　　　Whistle blows to rotate group to next Station (No.3)
5:15 to 5:30 Specific plays No.1 with Gp.3
　　　　　　　Whistle blows to gather for End of Practice
5:30 to 5:35 Short talk and closing ritual (All together)

Asst.No.2 Plus Assistant Station 3 (Up to 7 Kids)
4:40 to 4:55 Square Serving game with Gp.3
4:55 to 5:00 **Water Break** Whistle blows to start and end
　　　　　　　Whistle blows to rotate group to next Station (No.1)
5:00 to 5:15 Square serving game with Gp.2
　　　　　　　Whistle blows to rotate group to next Station (No.1)
5:15 to 5:30 Square serving game with Gp.1
　　　　　　　Whistle blows to gather for End of Practice
5:30 to 5:35 Short talk and closing ritual (All together)

Scheduling Summation

We have given you a bunch of different methods and ideas to help you make a schedule for your practice training. I know that many of you don't like to do this because I have talked to a lot of coaches over the years about scheduling. However, you need assistant coaches and parents to help you get better. If you can get them, you will see that things can go smoothly. You can also be innovative, and tailor the schedule to suit your own coaching style and techniques. There is almost an infinite amount of combinations you can have.

If your coaches don't like teaching the same thing for four straight 15 minute sessions, then mix it up and have each one of them teach something different at each 15 minute session at their station. However, tell them it is easier doing it three or six straight times because they don't need to change their court set up at every session. And they get a different group of kids each time, and each different group has their own challenges. So, if you don't like what I have shown then be innovative.

My only comment is don't try to do it all yourself. It does NOT work, especially if you have a big group. I hate when I happen to be out driving somewhere, and happen to see a big group of kids at something like a football practice just standing around waiting while coach only has one or two kids at a time over to the side trying to instruct them how to do something, and everyone else is just standing around doing nothing. In fact it does not even look like they are watching sometimes. There is a better way, if you will just try it.

THE END

CPSIA information can be obtained at www.ICGtesting.com
Printed in the USA
LVOW02s1506020514

384225LV00004B/9/P